Praise for Mary Helen Bowers and *Ballet Beautiful*:

"Ballet Beautiful completely transformed my body in a way I never thought possible. It toned and lengthened the muscles in my arms and legs and . . . eradicated cellulite and lifted and firmed my butt. I never thought I would comfortably wear short shorts again, but Ballet Beautiful changed that! The best part is it's so easy to maintain because I can do it from anywhere. Mary Helen Bowers is truly a body-sculpting magician. I could seriously go on forever about Ballet Beautiful—it is simply life-altering."

—Rachel Antonoff, designer

"Bowers, who developed a personal exercise routine from her own experience as a professional ballerina to create a demanding—and rewarding program that has attracted a roster of models and actresses, including Karen Elson."

—*Vogue*

"In the ten plus years I've been an editor at *Harper's Bazaar*, I've tried every exercise program imaginable, from complicated machines to simply sweating it out. But nothing—or no one—has transformed my body the way Mary Helen Bowers' Ballet Beautiful program has. Mary Helen's method garners results: long, lean muscle tone, better posture, a more controlled core. Mary Helen has made it impossible not to do Ballet Beautiful, whether it's her private sessions, group classes, on-line workouts or DVDs, so not only do I love how I look and feel, but I love that there are no excuses."

—Kristina O'Neill, executive editor, *Harper's Bazaar*

"I SWEAR to you that after my first class with Mary Helen my tight jeans that I usually have to wiggle myself into slid on with no problem."

—Tracee Ellis Ross, actress

"[T]he class strengthens and limbers the body through ballet-based movements."

—*New York* magazine

"Women have long coveted sinewy arms, high and tight derrieres, lean legs and a regal posture. Now, in search of this shape, many of them are ditching yoga and Pilates and lining up at the ballet barre. . . . At the front of the corps is Mary Helen Bowers, who trained Ms. [Natalie] Portman for the movie [*Black Swan*]."

—*The New York Times*

"All you need is enough space for a yoga mat . . . but the movements are designed to strengthen the muscles you would use if you were taking a ballet class."

—*Wall Street Journal*

"Shows off a celebrity fitness trend that could just be the next Pilates."

—*Publishers Weekly*

"The program definitely works . . . but feeling like a dancer in training is enough to keep us coming back for more."

—Gotham.com

"Ballerina Mary Helen Bowers . . . set the barre high."

—*Womens' Health*

BALLET BEAUTIFUL

BALLET
BEAUTIFUL

The fitness and lifestyle programme
to help any woman gain the strength, grace
and body of a ballet dancer

MARY HELEN BOWERS

Vermilion
LONDON

1 3 5 7 9 10 8 6 4 2

Published in 2012 by Vermilion, an imprint of Ebury Publishing
First published in the USA in 2012 by Da Capo Press, a member of the Perseus Books Group

Ebury Publishing is a Random House Group Company

BALLET BEAUTIFUL®

The Random House Group Limited Reg. No. 954009

Addresses for companies within the Random House Group can be found at
www.randomhouse.co.uk

A CIP catalogue record for this book is available from the British Library

The Random House Group Limited supports The Forest Stewardship Council (FSC®),
the leading international forest certification organisation. Our books carrying the FSC label are printed on
FSC® certified paper. FSC is the only forest certification scheme endorsed by the leading environmental
organisations, including Greenpeace. Our paper procurement policy can be found at
www.randomhouse.co.uk/environment

Photos by Yelena Yemchuk
Illustrations on pages 50–52 by Costanza Theodoli-Braschi
Design by Cynthia Young at Sagecraft
Printed and bound by CPI Group (UK) Ltd, Croydon, CR0 4YY

ISBN 9780091947583

Copies are available at special rates for bulk orders.
Contact the sales development team on 020 7840 8487 for more information.

To buy books by your favourite authors and register for offers, visit www.randomhouse.co.uk

Note: The information in this book has been compiled by way of general guidance in relation to the specific subjects addressed, but is not a substitute and not to be relied on for medical, healthcare, pharmaceutical or other professional advice on specific circumstances and in specific locations. Neither this diet and exercise programme nor any other diet and exercise programme should be followed without first consulting a health professional. If you have any special conditions requiring attention, you should consult with your health-care professional regarding possible modification of the programme contained in this book. So far as the author is aware the information given is correct and up to date as at March 2012. Practice, laws and regulations all change, and the reader should obtain up-to-date professional advice on any such issues. The author and publishers disclaim, as far as the law allows, any liability arising directly or indirectly from the use, or misuse, of the information contained in this book. The names and identifying details of people associated with events described in this book have been changed. Any similarity to actual persons is coincidental.

To my parents,
who taught me that no dream is ever out of reach,
and to my brothers, who taught me to be tough!

And to Paul,
a source of endless inspiration and love.

CONTENTS

FOREWORD

When I go to the ballet, I am always in awe of the dancers' bodies as much as I am of the beauty they express through movement: the definition in their arms, their strong legs, and the length—that beautiful line that extends from their fingertips to their toes, through their necks and torsos. I had the privilege of working with Mary Helen Bowers for a year in preparation for the film *Black Swan,* and her system works for nondancers by simplifying the balletic exercises that result in these beautiful lines.

Mary Helen's technique is based on the motions that ballerinas use all day long. It allows anyone to achieve the long, toned physique of a dancer. I had had essentially the same body since I was 14 years old, and after a couple of months working with Mary Helen it had been completely transformed. I gained length, strength, and tone. My arms and legs completely changed shape. My posture looked, as my dad said, like I had swallowed a broom. And it was all possible without equipment. For so many of us, with our transient lives and hectic schedules, the ability to do a workout at home with zero equipment is truly a gift.

My new regimen gave me a sense of discipline, a much better body image, and so much more strength, but in a way that always guarded against injury. Mary Helen's knowledge of healthy diet in conjunction with the exercises was also helpful in achieving the fitness goals we had set out. It was a truly comprehensive approach that allowed me to be physically convincing as a ballet dancer in a relatively short time. I hope that with this book you will also enjoy the insider knowledge that Mary Helen shares and learn how simply you too can attain the ballet body.

—*Natalie Portman*

LIVING BALLET BEAUTIFULLY

Artistic, Athletic, Attainable

Those three words have become my inspiration for the type of life I want to create, one that is healthy, fun, and full of possibility—not just for myself but for others. These words are close to my heart because they also represent the promise of Ballet Beautiful, a transformative approach to reshaping the body so that it becomes slender, long, and lean with the strength, grace, and elegant carriage of a ballerina. I used this method to train and prepare Natalie Portman for her Academy Award–winning role in *Black Swan*. I have also helped thousands of women around the world lose weight, turn fat into lean muscle, and recontour their bodies so that they too achieve the elegant posture and grace of a ballerina. The basis of my Ballet Beautiful program—and the book you now hold in your hands—is deeply connected to ballet's incredible artistry and rich yet mysterious tradition. Grace matched with strength is the essence of ballet and the inspiration for this program.

What makes this program remarkably unique is how it enables women, including myself, to embrace the emergence of their own inner beauty. Again and again, I have seen women incorporate my Ballet Beautiful method into their lives and then quite tangibly connect to a deep confidence. As Katherine, one of my longtime clients, told me, "Ballet Beautiful has allowed me to feel prettier than I ever thought possible."

With Ballet Beautiful, you too can attain and embody a truly feminine energy, poise, and power.

Achieving my dream of becoming a professional ballerina at age 16 was more challenging and more rewarding than I could ever have imagined. To create the Ballet Beautiful method I took all that is inspiring, strengthening, and empowering in ballet and its techniques and transformed it into a doable, streamlined system of movements that anyone can do at home, whether or not they have any dance training or experience. Of course, I didn't do that overnight. The end result is a product of my own trials and errors and what I've learned along the way. I developed the Ballet Beautiful method over the last 15 years as I gradually understood and then integrated all that I know about ballet, exercise, and nutrition into a comprehensive approach to life. Today Ballet Beautiful has become a total-body workout and lifestyle that allows anyone to achieve the toned, powerful body shape and beautiful posture of a ballerina.

As I began to craft and share my Ballet Beautiful method, I realized that one of the most important steps in achieving a physical transformation—in fact, what you have to do before any real and lasting change can take place—is to integrate a mindset that sets you up for success and helps you connect more deeply with your goals. This step is not as simple as giving yourself a pep talk. It is a strategy for implementing change, experiencing growth, and achieving something truly remarkable. I believe that there is incredible beauty, power, and grace in all of us and that it is possible to be both very feminine and very strong. This is the essence of Ballet Beautiful. With my program, I help women believe in themselves (as well as in the value of their dreams), envision themselves in a body and a life imbued with power and grace, and then achieve that goal. A shift to a healthier lifestyle happens organically with this new mindset, and anyone who practices it becomes truly Ballet Beautiful.

In the pages ahead, I will show you how to dig deep and really connect with this inherent part of yourself. I will show you how to attain the elegant silhouette and strength of a ballet dancer. And I will show you this in a fast-working program that you can do in the comfort and privacy of your own home.

Along with the exercises and mindset, I have also designed an approach to eating that has allowed me and my clients to feel satisfied and strong while also getting the best possible nutrition. This eating plan is filled with delicious, satisfying foods that will keep your metabolism humming and your body lean and strong. Ballerinas can be known for extreme discipline, even deprivation, when it comes to dieting. That approach does not work for me. My eating plan is based on a system of balance and contentment that supports health and weight loss so that any woman can achieve her ideal weight and then maintain it naturally.

Living Ballet Beautifully

The response to Ballet Beautiful has been tremendous! Thousands of women around the world have embraced this method, including some of today's most inspiring celebrities, A-list actresses, and supermodels in over 50 countries. One of the reasons Ballet Beautiful works so well for women in the spotlight is the same reason it will work for you—it lets you look incredible, feel healthy, and savor your femininity. With Ballet Beautiful, grace is both a physical and an emotional quality, a truly feminine balance of artistry and athleticism.

And the immediate results are incredibly motivating! In just one week, you will feel tighter and you may begin to see a change in how your clothes fit your body; in two weeks, your body's silhouette will be longer, leaner, and more toned. Over time, as your body responds to the program, these results become more dramatic:

- Your arms become taut and strong, not bulky.

- Your legs will be elongated, toned, and lean, not overly rounded by too much muscle.

- High and tight, your butt will be the perfect shape for wearing jeans . . . or a bathing suit.

- Your center will become narrow, flat, and strong.

- You'll see an elegance to your posture and carriage and feel an increased flexibility.

Many of my clients describe these results as being "immediate" and "addictive." The exercises are very targeted—you can feel them waking up your "ballet muscles" as you go. You will feel tighter and more pulled in after the first workout. You might even begin standing a little straighter too! I'll never forget when my friend told me about sliding into her tightest pair of skinny jeans with ease on the night of her first Ballet Beautiful workout. We've all had to dance our way into a pair of jeans before—just imagine the feeling of having them slide right on! Translation? Bring on Ballet Beautiful!

I relish the process of working hard for a true reward—witnessing the physical transformation of others through Ballet Beautiful is always very exciting to me! Our Facebook page has a wonderful community of Ballet Beauties celebrating their progress with the program and sharing incredible success stories. One fan recently commented, "I noticed a change in the definition in my arms after three days of doing Swan Arms!" Another hardworking fan wrote, "Hello Mary Helen and the Ballet Beautiful Community! I just had to tell you that I got my sister hooked on Ballet Beautiful and I can't wait for her to start seeing the kind of amazing results for her body that I've been seeing in my own! Thank you!!" I have clients who describe losing five pounds in the first week and others who see their transformation blossom over time as they tighten, tone, and elongate their muscles.

I work with a wide range of clients: women in their late thirties who want their bodies back after childbirth; forty-something women who have been so busy building their careers and taking care of kids (or not) that they haven't worked out in a decade; students and young models who wish to add muscle and definition to their lean frames; and women in their sixties who are fighting the effects of aging and staying youthful by strengthening their bones and muscles in a way that is not high-impact or stressful. In fact, one client in her midsixties who used the method while recovering from a shoulder injury said after four weeks, "I have never felt stronger! Ballet Beautiful has changed my life!"

Ballet Beautiful works for every woman because it is tied to the way the female body inherently moves, the inner lines of women's proportions, and the physiological structure of their form. I will show you how to use my ballet-inspired movements to strengthen your center and align your spine for better posture. I will help you cue into your joints and muscles as you do specific exercises to maximize the results, protect yourself from strain, and gain better body awareness.

These exercises are designed to target and define the sleek "ballet muscles" for every body type. There is no dancing involved, just focused, ballet-inspired exercises and stretches to strengthen and lengthen your body with very little impact. You will be able to transform your body and your mind in the privacy of your own home, getting to know the program with no interruptions and reaping all the benefits of a hundred private classes.

Ballet Beautiful is challenging, which is why the results are so incredible. The exercises work deep in your muscles, changing the shape of your figure from the inside out. I've designed the program in such a way that you can either work your body as a whole or break the sections down to target specific body parts or trouble spots (we all have them!), including arms, center, legs, and butt. Either way, the effect is the same: strong, lean, long muscles with improved flexibility and posture.

We will begin by working together to shift your mindset and connect to your intrinsic ability to make better choices and find a way to live the life of your dreams. Getting into the Ballet Beautiful mindset before we begin the workout is important because I want you to succeed! This shift in attitude will truly motivate you to take care of your body and treat it with respect, gentleness, and forgiveness—even as you power through my 15-Minute Butt Blast! The Ballet Beautiful mindset is about finding balance, listening to yourself and how you feel, and ultimately achieving satisfaction. Together these factors lay the groundwork for you to live Ballet Beautifully.

You will also learn to adapt to a simple yet wholesome way of eating that doesn't require overthinking; instead, you'll learn five principles to guide your food choices as you adjust how you eat to benefit weight loss (if that is what you desire) or support your body as it moves into its new Ballet Beautiful shape. You will feel stronger, and you will also feel more clear-headed, more energetic, and yes, even happier! As one woman, an incredibly talented up-and-coming artist, shared: "Through Ballet Beautiful, I discovered that I didn't need to be banging my body into the ground every day. I started thinking about life in terms of subtlety and longevity; lengthening my limbs instead of compressing them through hours of low-impact cardio. Now I feel graceful for the first time since I was a teenager, with boundless energy and confidence." Ballet Beautiful is more than just a workout or a diet—it is a state of mind.

Maybe you are frustrated with where you are or looking for ways to make changes, having tried and failed in the past. I will guide you toward your goal by helping you identify and uproot old patterns and bad behaviors. Ballet Beautiful will give you the tools to transform how you take care of yourself, making regular exercise and healthy eating rewarding and pleasurable parts of your daily life.

This program is flexible and designed to meet you exactly where you are, to help you define your goals, and to give you the inner resources to achieve all that you desire—for your body, your spirit, and your mind. Ballet Beautiful will also help you create more time and energy in your busy schedule for exercise and healthy meals. Once you fit Ballet Beautiful into your life, you too can achieve a sleek physique and become more efficient, productive, and energetic.

How the Book Works

This book is organized into three parts. Part I, "Building Your Ballet Beautiful Mindset," focuses on developing a mindset that will empower you and prepare you for incredible growth and change. I always say that Ballet Beautiful is more than just a workout—it's a way of living with grace, strength, and beauty. This state of being is the starting place for becoming Ballet Beautiful. With this mindset, you will tap into something greater than just a workout or a diet plan. Just as yoga is about more than just stretching, the positive Ballet Beautiful mindset teaches you to believe in yourself and all that you can accomplish. It also puts in place a system for setting clear goals so that you will never again look at obstacles or fixed behavior patterns in the same way.

If you feel stuck in an attitude that is blocking you, we will work together to shift that. If you need help identifying realistic, meaningful goals, we will do that too. These initial chapters lay the groundwork for the next two parts of the program.

Part II, "The Ballet Beautiful Program," introduces my approach to total-body fitness: the transformative exercises and stretches, the techniques behind them, and the targeted results they produce. The Ballet Beautiful method is made up of my Classic 60-Minute Workout and my 15-Minute Ballet Beautiful Blasts. Every exercise and stretch is influenced by my love for ballet and what I have learned about strengthening and sculpting the body. These are my own personal exercises. I would never share or suggest a movement that I would not use myself! The Blasts include four sets of exercises from my Cardio Series that are energizing and fun! All of the options provide incredible results and are designed to be customized so as to meet your body's needs and your schedule. You can create up to 25 different combinations of workouts—some that are only 15 minutes in length, others that are 30 minutes, others that are 45, and still others that can extend to 60 minutes. You will soon see that this program is inherently adaptable to your needs!

Part III, "The Ballet Beautiful Lifestyle," offers an approach to eating and living that is founded on the simplicity of great nutrition. If you are looking for something radical or extreme, you won't find it here. My own experiments with extreme dieting were far from positive. I lost weight, sure, but I was miserable. I also put the weight back on in the end. I learned a lot from this experience and now stay far away from extreme diets. This balanced approach is the foundation of the five lifestyle principles I developed to build on the mindset and show you how to eat well and be nourished, not just feed your body. These principles enable you to keep your mind and body in balance and make you feel grounded, satisfied, and centered in your life. **The five Ballet Beautiful lifestyle principles are:**

1. Be prepared.

2. Eat well and often.

3. Substitute for satisfaction.

4. Be flexible.

5. Forgive and move on.

The chapters in Part III give you the tools to put the mindset, the exercises, and the eating plan into motion and transform your lifestyle so that you strengthen and tone your body, lose weight, and stay in shape in a completely natural and effortless way. I will also give you a seven-day meal plan that makes it easy to shift to eating Ballet Beautifully, as well as my favorite delicious and easy-to-prepare recipes to enjoy along the way!

The secret to any successful approach to healthy eating and weight loss is satisfaction. I am adamant about the idea that only by finding satisfaction in how you eat can you achieve and maintain weight loss in a natural, healthy way. Here you will focus not on what you *cannot* eat, but rather on what you *can* eat. And you may be surprised by just how much that is! You won't be hungry or deprived because I'm not going to ask you to juice, fast, or practice drastic, low-calorie consumption. The Ballet Beautiful diet is a balanced diet, and it works!

I've included many easy-to-remember tips on how to shop and how to put together quick-and-easy meals using my "flash cooking" techniques and some delicious (but very simple!) recipes that make it easy and enjoyable to stick with this program. Rather than focusing on the negatives—using our energy to try to memorize or fantasize about long lists of forbidden foods—we'll focus on the positive. Together we will open doors to incredible possibilities and achieve a healthy new way of living.

I've designed this program for real people living busy, demanding lives. I take into account the pressures and difficulties of a modern life because I am living one too. Ballet Beautiful provides a flexible, portable, and attainable program for health, wellness, and fitness, even on days when you are short on time. With Ballet Beautiful, true transformation is possible, and that is something that I am very excited to share with you!

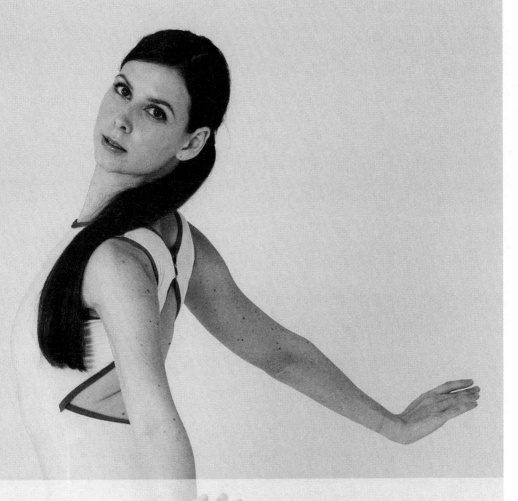

PART I

BUILDING YOUR BALLET BEAUTIFUL MINDSET

Health, fitness, and an ideal figure are attainable!

Chapter 1

The Genesis of Ballet Beautiful

My Story

As a little girl, I wanted nothing more than to become a ballerina. I danced everywhere I went, read every book on ballet I could find, and spent hours imagining what dancing as a ballerina in New York City might be like. My love for ballet has been a part of my life for just about as long as I can remember, and that remains true today. At the heart of the Ballet Beautiful program is the story of how my own experiences as a professional ballerina with the New York City Ballet led me to understand how to truly take care of myself—both my body and my mind—in how I live every day.

I began developing the fundamentals of the Ballet Beautiful method while recovering from an injury to my left foot early in my professional dance career. Because ballet is so physically demanding, I was used to dealing with pain in my body on a daily basis. I never really stopped to think about it. I adored dancing, and my focus was always on my performance; pain in my body was a minor and accepted irritation that I always found ways to work around. Blisters, strained muscles, and the terrible sensation of feeling the floor with your toes in a dying pair of pointe shoes are all de rigueur for a professional ballerina—not to mention incredible stress from the constant fear that an injury will prevent you from taking the stage that night. In the world of ballet, managing these physical demands while remaining strong and healthy onstage is just part of the job.

During an early season with the New York City Ballet that was particularly busy and rewarding for me, I was dancing three ballets a night, six days a week, on top of ballet class every morning and a full day of rehearsals. These were long, hard, but also very happy days. I was dancing all of my favorite Balanchine ballets, including *Donizetti Variations, Mozartiana, Serenade,* and stark, neoclassical leotard ballets that have no story lines, fluffy tutus, or sets and whose focus is on the dancing and music only, like *Episodes, The Four Temperaments,* and *Le Tombeau de Couperin.* Performing this repertoire was artistic heaven. Almost nightly I danced a selection of the greatest ballets ever created, onstage at Lincoln Center. Life was almost perfect for me. As an artist, my soul was full! But over the course of the season, the grueling schedule began to take its toll on my body.

I was in constant pain. I wrapped my foot during rehearsals and for the shows, but no amount of tending helped me heal—I was often barely able to walk in the hours before the curtain went up or the next morning when I awoke.

As my injury progressed, it took more and more effort to rehearse and perform through the pain. I had to will myself to ignore the strong signals my body was sending me to take time off; sheer will and adrenaline carried me through every performance. In this way ballet can be like an addictive drug—I found it very hard to take time off even when I knew that continuing to dance was hurting me. The pain didn't take away my urge to dance and perform. If anything, it magnified that desire and made it stronger as I considered what my life would be like without ballet.

Night after night the curtain fell, and I limped offstage and upstairs to the dressing room to cut off the ribbons on my pointe shoes and dunk my feet in ice. Finally, after weeks of pushing myself beyond my limits, I had to admit that my injury had become a serious problem. No dancer wants to leave the stage, however, and surrender her roles to another. Ballet is a very competitive world—there is always someone waiting in the wings to step in. I wasn't happy about the idea that my physical weakness might alter or threaten my career and that other girls might get the chance to dance my hard-won parts.

Trying not to panic, I gave in to the reality of my injury when I realized that no amount of ice, ibuprofen, or warming up before a show would allow me to perform. I had been living on my own in New York City since I was 15 years old, and I worried about how to get the right care for my foot and how to manage the stress of being replaced by another dancer while I was recovering. After I went to the doctor and was fitted for a giant boot, I stopped performing, taking class, and rehearsing every day. I began to focus on healing instead.

After a significant rest period, I was ready to get back in shape. I joined a health club in New York and started experimenting with exercise and training my body outside of a dance studio for the first time. I was worried about having taken off so much time, and it was hard to imagine being in good enough condition to perform again. I began trying different fitness classes and machines, always looking for a way to make the exercises work on my body as a dancer. I couldn't risk overdeveloping my muscles or dramatically changing my shape. In a kickboxing class, I did jumping jacks to a grand plié in second position, never lifted weights heavier than three or five pounds, kept perfect ballet posture and included tons of stretching between exercises and sets. As I began to notice that working outside of a ballet studio made a difference in my performance ballet class, I discovered the incredible benefits of cross-training as my body got stronger. Old aches and pains in my knees and tendons went away, and soon I was performing at a higher level. Inspired, I began experimenting in my free time with creating new targeted exercises to build endurance and strength and to develop the muscles I needed for peak performance as a ballet dancer. It was a pivotal discovery, and the genesis for what became the Ballet Beautiful method.

Initially, I created core exercises in the Ballet Beautiful method as a way to support my healing, but as my foot recovered I soon realized that the workout I had devised for myself enabled me to return to the stage a completely different dancer: I was stronger, leaner, and more in touch with my body than ever before. Whereas before I danced with confidence in my technique, I now danced with a new confidence in my body, a confidence that felt almost effortless. I am grateful for the longevity that this workout gave me in a physically punishing career that can be frightfully short.

Several years later, after ten years of dancing with the New York City Ballet, I made the really hard decision to retire from the company to pursue my degree at Columbia University and other interests outside of dance. This decision was difficult because of what ballet means to me. I have a very deep love for ballet that is hard to explain. I can only tell you that I feel as if ballet is what I was born to do and that every step in my life up to that point had propelled me toward dancing with the New York City Ballet. We were fated to be together! It was painful to leave the stage that I loved so much and worked so hard to dance on every night. But I had also begun to listen to another part of myself that wanted more balance, new forms of expression, and intellectual challenges.

I was also growing tired of the constant sacrifice that ballet requires. My childhood was very normal and happy—my mom is a retired children's librarian, and my father is an accountant. I went to public school in Charlotte, North Carolina, before moving to New York to attend the School of American Ballet (the official school of the New York City Ballet) at age fifteen. Even though I have always had this wild and almost inexplicable love for ballet, I have also always known that somehow there would be more for me than dance. I certainly didn't know what that meant when I retired from the company, or how ballet would remain an important part of my life down the road. Even as part of me mourned the loss of my dancing career and my beloved stage, another part delighted in the adventure ahead. I was finally ready to experience new challenges, set new goals, and discover a world and identity for myself beyond the stage.

I thought that making such a radical change might leave me feeling empty or depressed. The opposite happened: I was thrilled! After so many years of living and breathing ballet, I loved having freedom in my daily schedule and a blank slate for my future just waiting to be written. It was scary, for sure, but liberating too. And one of my first challenges was learning how to relax and enjoy myself as I focused on my studies and began building a new life.

When I started at Columbia University, I was ready for a break. I took a year off from dancing and working out to rest my body and my mind. I let this happen naturally—I didn't want to work out and I did not push myself to. It came as no surprise when, without the daily workouts, my body softened and I got out of shape. I had to buy new clothes and jeans to fit my new curvy form. When I felt ready to start moving again, I did not want to go to the gym or back to ballet class. I didn't freak out—I just went with those feelings and decided to back off and work out at home.

Slowly, I returned to the workout method that I had devised for my old injury, making adjustments as I went. Because my figure had changed, I was uncomfortable around other dancers. I enjoyed the privacy and solitude of working out at home. In my new life as a full-time student, not only did I drop the extra pounds, I got into the best shape of my life. As I developed new body awareness, I made changes in a slow and steady way, experimenting with what my body needed, noticing how it responded to certain exercises, foods, and lifestyle choices. With no pressure to don a leotard and tights, I was able to take my time and think through my workout systematically. Because I was doing it just for me, I felt happy and excited when I would see a change. The workout became once again a program that was all about making my body fitter, stronger, and more efficient, not about having to look a certain way. I didn't have to feel bad about gaining weight or wasting money on the gym.

This was a very creative time. Without any pressure or expectations, I refined the movements and added new exercises, tweaked my diet, and made adjustments as I went along. But what was truly remarkable was how good I felt—as if I had discovered a hidden secret. I had figured out how to take the strength, grace, and artistry of ballet—the elements of dance that I cherish and that I missed the most in my daily life—and apply them to my life outside of Lincoln Center. The results were amazing. I found myself more focused and confident, more energetic and productive. I began looking forward to my at-home workouts as a way to take some time just for me rather than as a punishment for having overeaten or as a boring, tedious chore. I also realized over time that my body was in better shape than it had ever been when I was dancing full-time—all without stepping inside a ballet studio. As I became leaner, more toned, and more confident, my friends and family wanted to know why!

Innovation and adaptability have always been an important part of Ballet Beautiful, at its inception and to this day. I began to share the program I'd developed with friends and fellow students at Columbia, and word of mouth took it from there. Women looking for a different approach to fitness, including actors and performers, high-profile working women, models, and celebrities began seeking me out. I officially launched Ballet Beautiful after graduating from Columbia. When I was later presented with the opportunity to travel to prepare Natalie Portman for *Black Swan,* my business in New York was really taking off. I would be away from my New York–based clientele for a significant period of time and needed to be able to stay connected to my clients no matter where I had to travel, so I developed a way to work with my students in an innovative online classroom, transporting Ballet Beautiful to wherever my students were—and wherever I was. I had to reexamine my location-based business model and think hard about scale in order to keep my business alive and growing. I leapt with delight into the rather unexpected role of technology entrepreneur as I began creating my own software for interactive, online training via my website, *www.balletbeautiful.com*. I love the way that my online classes also reflect the classic Ballet Beautiful ideals—they are portable, flexible, and cutting-edge. This is the future of fitness, and I'm proud to play a role in developing it!

And the rest is history!

. . .

For me, Ballet Beautiful is about the process of overcoming obstacles and achieving dreams. Whether it is recovering from an injury, finding a healthier approach to food, or creating a way to share Ballet Beautiful with women all over the world and stay connected with my clients when I am on the road, I have learned that having a smart, systemized approach and mindset is everything. I've also learned that anything is truly possible within the principles of Ballet Beautiful! I feel incredibly fortunate to have first achieved my dream of becoming a ballerina in New York City at such a young age. Now I am excited to share my dream of taking all that I have discovered in Ballet Beautiful and sharing it with you. Through Ballet Beautiful, you too can attain the artistry and athleticism of a dancer and embrace your own inner beauty. You too can become Ballet Beautiful.

Chapter 2

Mindset

The Key to Health, Happiness, and Success

Though I was born with a natural gift for dance, my mindset has always been a work in progress. For this program, mindset is key: it is the way you approach your life. It is your inner voice that helps you shape your goals and imagine your dreams. It's your attitude about yourself and your capabilities, a reflection of how you see the world around you. Mindset is also the part of you that kicks in when you have to overcome an obstacle or solve a problem, and ultimately it is your mindset that keeps you on course to succeed. Your mindset is a compass for living your life, a critical inner guide to achieving your full potential and reaching your wildest dreams.

As a dancer, your body is everything. Every exercise, stretch, step, and gesture is thought about, measured, and calculated to make you look your most beautiful, elegant, ethereal. But what about the way you feel? Your mindset can be hard to define: it is both emotional and intellectual, and it has a physical meaning as well.

Why is mindset important? Because it is the crucial piece connecting your body to your mind, allowing not only my Ballet Beautiful program but your life to work for you as a harmonious whole.

When I was younger, the connection between my body and my mind was completely natural; I think that is probably true for many of us. I ate when I was hungry, drank when I was thirsty, and danced because it made me happier than anything else in the world. I didn't think about all the pieces because my life was working so well naturally! But as I got older and began absorbing some of the destructive behavior of the girls around me at the theater, I lost this natural connection to my body and the way I ate. As a ballerina, I felt a lot of pressure to be perfect, and sometimes that took its toll.

Even though I came to understand the importance of training my body outside of a dance studio, my diet was a mess. It took time for me to connect how I felt with some of my not-so-healthy behaviors. With a lot of patience, introspection, and willingness, I began to understand the impact that my mindset had on my body. When my body was off key, more often than not my mindset was somehow standing in the way, preventing me from performing at my best and treating my body with the love and care it deserved. As I tuned in to my mindset, I started to realize that my metabolism had slowed down because I wasn't always eating enough, or that I didn't necessarily need to train 70 hours a week in a ballet studio to be in terrific ballet shape.

These connections made me realize that having a limiting mindset can produce a negative outcome, and that a positive, forgiving, and very open mindset helps me relax and better connect to my body. Learning this has been very empowering, and it has totally changed my life.

It's been a process of discovery, and I can tell you firsthand that before you begin the Ballet Beautiful movements or change the way you eat, it's crucial that you become aware of your mindset so that you can truly believe in yourself, your future, and your ability to change. It will make a world of difference in the results.

Expanding My Horizons

It wasn't until I retired from the New York City Ballet and stopped dancing every day that I fully realized how much more I needed in my life to feel complete.

I loved finding another intense way to express myself as I transitioned into a full-time student at Columbia University—reading and discussing great literary works of art with fellow students provided a new way to find that balance. By changing my environment and daily patterns, I was able to begin building a new identity on top of the old. My time at Columbia helped me find a way to express myself verbally and intellectually that was really a relief. It was nice not to depend only on my body for my art. With ballet, I often felt like a body without a voice.

I took time to relish my freedom, relaxing into a new schedule that did not begin each morning in the dance studio and end onstage. I could go to the movies, stay up late, see and hang out with my friends for longer than a half-cup of coffee, or even sneak away for a long weekend with my boyfriend. Because I wasn't dancing in more than 45 shows of *The Nutcracker* each December, or training up to 70 hours each week, I now could travel home to North Carolina to see my family for the holidays. I instinctively knew that I needed a serious break from the ballet world, for my body and my mind. I stopped dancing and working out altogether, giving my body a chance to rest, recover, and find a new normal. My shape changed, my muscles softened, and I put on weight. I ate and enjoyed foods that I had once thought were forbidden.

As the months passed and I began adjusting to my life as a student, I began to slowly realize that I missed the connection that I had always had with my body. My body craved movement, and when my mind felt ready again, I started slowly and didn't put pressure on myself to get to the gym. As I began getting back into shape, I began to clarify my understanding of the power of mindset and what it could do for me.

I figured out that what I wanted was to work at my own pace from home, without the pressure of others around me. So several days a week, I would lay down a towel or a

Katherine on Mindset

I love the fact that Ballet Beautiful fits so easily into my life. If I don't have an hour, I do shorter, 15-minute Blasts throughout the day. I maintain my strength but, more importantly, I don't lose my momentum and get discouraged. Because Ballet Beautiful is accessible in so many different ways and in many varying time increments, I always fit it in. It feels good to accomplish something every day, be it big or small, toward my goal of staying healthy and strong.

yoga mat in my apartment, picking up again with the exercises and stretches I had created for myself while dancing with the New York City Ballet. After spending 10 years dancing 12 hours a day, 6 days a week, I was amazed to see my body's response to this new workout program that took just 45 minutes a day. My muscles came back, tightening and toning up even as I was eating foods I had once thought to be off limits—pasta, dark chocolate, cheese. I was doing things differently, exploring a new way of working out for the first time, and seeing my life through a new lens, one that was forgiving and positive. With my previous mindset, this would not have been possible. Because I was developing a mindset that was flexible, and giving myself the opportunity to take a break and start over, I was able to create Ballet Beautiful, but this did not happen overnight. I spent a lot of time making mistakes and figuring out exactly what worked for my body and, even more importantly, my mind.

If we are open to it, life is full of those moments—big and small—and they offer incredible possibility for growth.

Developing Your Mindset and Trusting Yourself

Developing the right mindset is not just about being positive or putting on a happy face. Have you decided to try my program because you just want to learn how to cut out a few calories so you can lose a few pounds? You should know right now that building your Ballet Beautiful mindset is both simpler and more profound than that.

When your mindset is positive and empowering, you trust yourself. You also learn to believe in your own ability to reach a goal, no matter how difficult that goal may seem or how many times you may have failed in the past. When you're feeling negative or doubt yourself, no matter how much you want to make a change, some part of you will undermine your goals and stop you from believing that real change, progress, and personal success are possible. How do you learn to overcome bad habits, negative thoughts and behavioral patterns that seem impossible to change? You face them head on. You reflect on yourself, dig deep, and learn to set clear, simple goals that you adjust along the way to reinforce your own success.

Developing a mindset that will sustain and empower you to change is ultimately about learning to believe that, yes, you do deserve the health, beauty, and grace you desire. Let's start with a few simple questions:

1. Why did you pick up this book?

2. Do you feel inspired to change the way your body looks and feels?

3. Do you feel inspired to change the way you feel about your body and your health?

These are three simple but important questions to keep in mind as you think about beginning the Ballet Beautiful program. You may even want to write down both the questions and your responses. At first, the answers to these questions may seem obvious, but if you take a moment, you will find a subtle power to them. Sometimes we rush through the busyness of our days, bothered by how we look or how we feel in our clothes. We have racing but fleeting thoughts such as, *If only I could lose 10 pounds!* or *I have to get in better shape!* There is nothing wrong with these thoughts; they are perfectly normal. But if you don't take the time to stop and consider them more specifically, you can unknowingly set yourself up for failure. You might rush out to buy the latest diet pill or the magazine offering a program that promises a weight loss of 10 pounds in two weeks, skip meals to cut calories, or you may overeat later. In our longing to get to the finish line, we often look for a quick fix—which 9 times out of 10 only leads to failure.

The bottom line is simple: extreme dieting and working out is unnecessary punishment. It ultimately hurts your body and mind and distances you from positive goals.

Sure, a cabbage diet may make you lose the promised 10 pounds, but can you maintain it? The return to normal (that is, regular eating) after an extreme diet is punishing; the pounds come back at record speed, leaving you frustrated and angry. This sort of behavior and your body's response is incredibly damaging to both your body and your mind. So how do you turn thoughts about your body and food into constructive behavior when you no longer have that natural relationship? You develop and rely on a more positive mindset and trust that your natural relationship with your body, food, and eating will follow.

I have used determination, focus, and a belief in my dreams and goals to create my program, and now I'd like to inspire you to embrace this empowering lifestyle for yourself. When I started using this approach in my own life, everything changed. In the past I might have thought about and obsessed over how I *looked*. Now I am interested in how I *feel*. Looking good doesn't mean much unless you feel happy, balanced, and satisfied.

Jenna on Mindset

Doing Ballet Beautiful makes me feel like a far more balanced person. I've become a lot more positive. I also feel like I've become more feminine through the process. I've been an athlete all my life, and I even walk differently now—Ballet Beautiful has changed my walk! I feel more confident, a little lighter—like I'm floating!

What does your mindset come down to? An attitude premised on growth, change, and a belief that working hard will help you to live better. Without this mindset, any exercise or diet program will fail. In short, you can't truly have strength, grace, and elegance on the outside if you don't cultivate it on the inside.

TUNE OUT THE NEGATIVE VOICES, TUNE IN TO YOU

Have you ever found yourself thinking, *My body has changed . . . I'm getting older . . . My metabolism just isn't what it used to be . . . I hate my body . . . I have no self-control?*

All of these negative statements are attached to a voice that you don't want to listen to as you plan your goals and set out to achieve them. There is no room for this undermining rant in your Ballet Beautiful life.

This voice could be the one that tells you to eat the extra scoop of ice cream because you are already fat so what does it matter. Or maybe the voice is a reflection of an emotional injury from years ago that is still tied to your self-esteem. Whatever its source, this voice could doom you to failure.

I had to work hard to learn to tune out negativity in my own life, so I appreciate how hard this can be. One year when I had a long break between the ballet summer and the winter season, I ended up gaining some weight. I was heavier than usual when I returned to class and rehearsals. By my first onstage rehearsal for *The Nutcracker*

I hadn't lost the weight, and I was feeling really self-conscious about it. While stretching out backstage after that rehearsal, I was told that I had been cut. I was horrified, devastated. And totally humiliated. I didn't know what I would tell my family visiting for the shows or my friends, or even how I would face the other dancers in the company. It was definitely a low point. I did end up losing the weight and was back onstage for *The Nutcracker* that year. But I also struggled with my self-image and felt obsessed with my weight for a time. I had to learn to separate my weight from my self-worth to get to a healthier place. I also had to realize that at the end of the day the way I treat myself makes the biggest difference in how I look and feel. That's true for all of us.

When someone tells you—or you tell yourself—that you aren't good enough, capable enough, smart enough, thin enough, curvy enough, or whatever enough, it can be hard to stay focused on the good and tune out the bad. Negative voices can dwell in your head and mix with your own voice. They are fueled by self-doubt, insecurity, and fear and can only lead to more of the same. They are also your worst enemy when you are trying to reach your goals and build a happy, healthy life for yourself. Indeed, if you listen to these negative voices, they can prevent you from reaching your goals—every time.

By simply becoming aware of the negative voices in your head and remembering that in fact they come from the outside, not from within, you can begin to take away their power. Try this out next time you hear yourself saying anything negative about your body or the way you look, feel, or behave:

- **Pause** and take a moment to think about what you've just said.

- **Think** about why you said that and why you are feeling that.

- **Remind yourself** that you are capable.

- **Shift your focus** to a challenge that you recently met successfully, whether in Ballet Beautiful or not.

- **Take a moment** to remember and reconnect to your belief that you can achieve your goals.

Silencing the negative and empowering the positive takes awareness and practice, but over time you will learn to set down new thought patterns based on all that you can do, not on any of your shortfalls that may or may not exist.

Together, we can work to replace negative, destructive voices with positive, encouraging, and challenging thoughts about yourself, your life, and your body! This is how we put the Ballet Beautiful mindset to work.

The Ballet Beautiful mindset is all about empowerment! Living Ballet Beautiful is not just about modifying your diet or executing the exercises—though obviously those are core features of the program. To maximize the ballet-inspired movements as well as tone and reshape your body through dietary changes, you must make sure that your inner attitude—your self-orientation—is pointing you in the direction of success.

By avoiding the pitfalls of yo-yo dieting and crash courses on fitness, you will reinforce the belief that you can make and maintain changes, that you trust yourself to reach your goals, and that you see yourself in the new body you desire. By developing a belief in yourself and in the program you are embarking on, you will be able to make true changes and accomplish this new way of life.

You will need to take the following steps to shift your inner voice from one that can paralyze you with self-criticism and doubt to one that empowers you instead to accept and then embrace your ability to rise to any occasion, persist in the face of any obstacle, and forgive yourself and move on even if you down a pint of ice cream. Remember: *You can shift your mindset and change your life!*

1. Can you bring to mind a situation that you dreaded before it happened, and sure enough, your worst fears were realized? Perhaps it was a work meeting, a job interview, or even a date that went just as badly as you had imagined it would.

2. Do you think that experience would have been different if you had approached it with a mindset that left what happened open-ended?

3. Can you remember a time when you avoided a challenge rather than take the chance of failing?

4. Can you now imagine embracing that same challenge *because you are less afraid to fail or make a mistake?*

5. Can you think of a time when you encountered an obstacle to a plan, project, or goal and felt like giving up? Maybe you were on a strict diet and had to go to a party; maybe you were trying to change jobs and you were turned down for a position.

6. How might you prepare for such an opportunity now, knowing that all endeavors involve certain obstacles or challenges? Do you think you might be able to prepare for challenges by trusting your ability to overcome them?

It's not always easy shifting away from a mindset that is premised on fear and the belief that certain outcomes are preordained. But it is possible. No one is perfect. And one of the secret weapons of the Ballet Beautiful mindset is its inherent flexibility and forgiveness, which is why I suggest staying away from any extremes. Ballet Beautiful is a challenging, targeted workout with a culture that is demanding yet relaxed. As a woman, I love this mix! I love being challenged, but I don't like being forced—this is a great combination that always makes me motivated and leaves me wanting more. As you will soon see, you can do the workout twice a week, three times, or even six times; it's up to you and how fast you want to see results. I'm not asking you to make impossible sacrifices or deprive yourself of food. As your priorities shift, the way you make decisions will too: you will make the time to eat well and exercise, but it will no longer feel like a burden. You won't feel like you're making huge sacrifices and depriving yourself. The changes will reinforce the shift in attitude as you begin to get results. In fact, you will feel like you're giving yourself a gift—every day.

I have so many clients who for years resented or even hated working out; in their minds working out had been a chore. But Ballet Beautiful is going to feel like a reward to yourself—something you miss when you can't do it!

As you start to make changes and shift your behavior, it is incredibly helpful to surround yourself with people who support you and will cheer you on. This doesn't happen automatically, and it may be a bit more complicated than it sounds. In fact, some of your friends and family may actually withdraw or feel threatened as you begin to change, shift, and grow. They might make negative or unsupportive comments. You can probably expect some resistance from people around you when you really start to shine. Don't take it personally. Some people see change in others as a threat to themselves or their lifestyle, which may not be the healthiest. Part of the Ballet Beautiful mindset is learning to live your life to the fullest without letting the negativity of others (or yourself!) set you back. How do you handle this when it happens? You build a strong community around yourself, and you also build strength within yourself to keep you on track.

Over the next few weeks, you will begin to shift your mindset and connect to your intrinsic ability to make better choices and find a way to live the life of your dreams. But the very next step is setting goals that are clear and achievable. The Ballet Beautiful community will be here to cheer you on!

Setting Your Ballet Beautiful Goals

I am a very goal-oriented person. I love having goals to work toward and delight in working with clients toward their own goals—be it getting ready for a wedding, embarking on a postnatal program, preparing for an onscreen role, or just getting ready for bikini season. Setting and working toward a goal can be an incredibly rewarding process. Ballet Beautiful is all about empowerment, remember? There is nothing more empowering than achieving your goals, be they large or small! Ballet Beautiful goal setting will lead you to that inner place where you can finally accomplish what it is you really want. I can't overestimate the importance of setting simple goals—it's one of the keys to being Ballet Beautiful!

When it comes to your health and the decision to create true and lasting change in your lifestyle, goal setting is one of your most important inner tools. Without it, you risk getting lost and tripped up by obstacles along the way, or experiencing the pain of helplessly watching your hard-won achievements slip away as you regain weight you had lost suddenly (or not so suddenly). Ballet Beautiful goal setting can prevent these kinds of disappointments and keep you on track.

Goal setting with Ballet Beautiful will help you sync up with your mindset, align your actions with your desires, and help ensure your success with the program! As you learn to connect to your goals, you cultivate an inner resource that can center and guide you, even when life becomes hectic and unpredictable. Life is guaranteed to surprise you; it's important to have a system that can see you through.

Here you'll discover simple tips and checklists for setting and meeting your goals for better fitness and a healthier diet and lifestyle. Whether your goal is to lose 10 pounds or 20, to wear your clothes with more confidence, or simply to feel stronger, cleaner, and brighter, you will find easy ways to match your most important desires to goals that are completely achievable.

And this is true whether or not you've ever pointed your toe or taken a ballet class. My program is designed for any woman, any body, and any level of dance experience . . . even a complete lack of it. It's very important to keep this in mind so that as you become familiar with the movements you don't expect to execute certain motions as if you've trained in ballet for 20 years!

It's a Process

Determining and realizing your goals is not as simple as naming a desired outcome. If goal setting were as easy as making a wish, we would all already be living an idyllic life at our ideal shape, weight, and size. I am not saying that this isn't possible, so please don't misunderstand. To the contrary! I believe that every woman has the ability to transform her body and her life so that she can embody a shape that matches her inner ideal. However, I have learned along the way that for my clients and myself, goal setting involves a lot of hard but also incredibly rewarding work.

I love this process because it is literally the path to achieving your dreams and anyone can do it. It's a process that requires that you be truly honest with yourself about your strengths as well as your vulnerabilities. To do that you have to look deep inside to understand what makes you tick, what makes you feel motivated, and what makes you want to quit. Effective goal setting is one part formula and one part self-awareness, and it is definitely not one size fits all. You have to learn to listen and trust yourself and your instincts in this process; they will rarely guide you in the wrong direction.

Remember when I was getting started again with Ballet Beautiful as a student at Columbia? My body was telling me that I wanted to work out, but my mind didn't want to go to the gym. Tuning in and listening to a need (even one that I didn't fully understand) to work out from home let me accomplish everything I needed—that is one of the key ideas embedded in the Ballet Beautiful method. So trust yourself and do what your body needs now—knowing that these needs will always change. Goal setting is as individual as your taste in clothes or food.

Ultimately, goal setting requires effort and perseverance so that each day you feel yourself moving toward your goal. This is good! Don't be scared of working hard on this part of yourself, because once you arrive the rest of it happens easily without too much planning or effort. Part of the beauty of goal setting is this very process—it is a wonderful chance to learn about yourself, to observe why you may have experienced failure in the past, and to find solace, new strength, and a belief in yourself and your capabilities.

Maybe you are frustrated with where you are or looking for ways to make changes. That's okay. This program is essentially flexible and designed to meet you exactly where you are, help you define your goals, and give you the inner resources to achieve all that you desire—for your body, your spirit, and your mind.

Ballet Beautiful will help you create more time and energy in your busy schedule. My days are incredibly busy running and building my company—I understand how challenging it is to find time to work out! I also realize how lucky I am to be able to sneak in a workout with my clients when I am teaching class, and I know that my body aches when I spend too much time at my desk or in a car. I am in the same predicament as any woman trying to balance a career with family time and personal time. I find this balance by making cuts in other areas of my life: I file my own nails instead of getting a manicure, I don't blow-dry my hair, and I only wear mascara when I'm going to a fancy dinner or being photographed! If I need a facial, I'll just do a face mask while I catch up on email. This leaves me some extra time to work out and to buy and prepare healthy food, which I make a priority. The truth is that we just can't do it all, but setting the right priorities will go a long way toward getting the right things done!

Gabrielle on Goal Setting

My goal setting started really simply: all I set out to do was commit to the program three days a week. I felt like this amount of time was a realistic commitment. I knew from the other women that I would see a difference doing the workout, so it wasn't intimidating. I wanted to commit to it and do it no matter how hard it was and to let it change me. Since I am not a dancer, part of my goal was not to let stereotypes about who can and can't do ballet hold me back and inform my choices. I immediately saw changes in my body and started to get great feedback from people on how I looked! I gained confidence and now do it as much as I can!

Make the Commitment and Clarify Your Goal

Have you found yourself setting out to lose weight and be healthier, only to get frustrated with your body and yourself time and again? I know so many women who have tried diets and extreme exercise programs, often with no lasting success. And what happens? They are left with a sense of futility and lack of control and a belief that they really cannot transform their bodies. Or they cling to extremes like juicing and fasting because those practices worked in the past.

This frustration is common among women who have not been working out for a while and who set out to lose weight or get in shape with nonstop dieting and exercise, only later to crash and burn. Or it happens to women who set their sights on losing 10 or 20 pounds and then, after a couple of weeks of total dedication to eating right and working out, they have a bad day, skip their workout, and in an instant lose the will to make better choices at dinner, followed by more bad choices at breakfast the next day. Before they know it, they have lost all momentum. They quit. They despair. They totally lose faith. And not just faith in their program, but in themselves. Sound familiar?

I have been there before, and it is not a good place. I have gained weight and experienced frustration because my body wasn't responding the way I wanted. But when I look back now, I see that my frustration stemmed from not looking at the big picture and considering my health and happiness; I was obsessing over how I could make a change fast, whether it was looking thinner in a leotard or getting into a tight pair of jeans. I didn't realize that my flash dieting was destroying my once-swift metabolism and throwing everything out of whack. It wasn't until I took a step back that it all started to make sense. I also realized that when it came to goal setting, the solution wasn't going to appear overnight.

In most cases, we fail to achieve weight or fitness goals because the goal we set at the very beginning was unrealistic, unhealthy, or lacking in the structure needed to ensure success. Our motivation or inspiration breaks down because our goals were not specific enough to sustain or were not healthy in nature. For example, if your motivation to change your diet includes a plan to cheat on "off days" later on, you should not expect lasting results. Being kind to yourself and giving yourself a rest day is good for you, but restricting calories with the goal of cheating (i.e., overeating or bingeing on unhealthy foods) only undermines your goals and your mindset. It's hard on your body too. A goal that is not clear and simple often becomes more of a wish; you just are not committed in the same way. Without this clarity, people often lose motivation and stop trying.

The great news is that when you are clear about your goal, identify it, and then map out the steps to get you there, you learn to truly believe in your goal and you work hard to meet it. This is what success looks like—it's the little things that you do every single day that impact the big picture and get you where you want to be.

True change doesn't happen overnight and that's okay! It's always better to go a little more slowly and have the results really stick, especially when it comes to your health. I recommend crafting a realistic breakdown of markers in time—stay on track by thinking about where you want to be after two weeks, after one month, after three months, and after six months and beyond.

I'm not telling you to set your sights low—if there is one thing I hate to hear it is *Take it slow* or *Don't aim too high!* Do not ever underestimate your brilliance, your capability, your smarts. And don't let the limiting vision or point of view of others define your concept of yourself. Defy them and enjoy the process of meeting your Ballet Beautiful goals!

Here are some questions that may guide you in defining your goals:

1. Is there an area of your body that you would like to transform?

2. Is there an area of your body that you would like to strengthen or lengthen? (These two go hand in hand!)

3. Do you have an ideal weight for your body type and general metabolism? If you'd like to lose weight, it's important to be realistic. It's safest and most successful to aim for one to two pounds a week. So if you want to lose 10 pounds, plan on achieving this in five weeks or more; if it's 20 pounds you'd like to lose, plan on 10 weeks; and so on.

4. Do you want to fit exercise into your daily life so that you will have more energy, develop more focus for work or projects during the day, and sleep better at night? Then it's important to plan out and commit to your program, scheduling your Ballet Beautiful into your week.

You can have multiple goals at the same time. But it's important to be clear on what those goals are and match specific actions to meet them. For some, making more than one change at once is overwhelming; others enjoy the intensity of making more global changes. It's up to you—you know yourself best.

Focus on Your Results for Motivation

One of the most motivating features of the Ballet Beautiful program is its results! I have seen again and again how empowered and encouraged women feel when their bodies begin to lengthen and transform. I encourage my clients to commit at least three days a week to my program because that commitment allows enough time for the body to show real results in just a matter of weeks.

Gabrielle remarked, "I saw initial change after two to three weeks. I noticed that I was stronger and my body was tighter. After one month, I saw even more dramatic changes around my waist and hips. My entire center became more tight and toned, along with my inner thighs, butt, and hips—all areas I was missing with traditional exercise regimes. I had been spending so much time in the gym working out, but I never felt like I was getting anywhere. Suddenly, I was experiencing all of these changes in my body doing Ballet Beautiful just three days a week!"

Katherine also noticed fast changes and explained how these changes motivated her. "I think that the immediate changes you see with Ballet Beautiful push you harder. Seeing results in just two weeks of starting the program really propelled me to keep doing the workout. I'm not an avid exerciser by nature, so this was really encouraging!"

Jenna's experience doing Ballet Beautiful was slightly different. As a tall, athletic powerhouse, she was looking for different changes:

"I love Ballet Beautiful. I feel that I've become a far more balanced person. My posture has definitely improved. I've been an athlete all my life, but I tend to add bulk very easily. Since starting the program, I see my muscles elongating. Ballet Beautiful allows for femininity without losing strength."

Your goals will reflect your needs—and no one else's!

What Do You Want?

Does this seem like a difficult question? It can stall the best of us. Many of us feel over-whelmed when we think about what we want, and that clouds our view as we try to an-swer this question. I think this question can be particularly difficult for women who are inclined to take care of others before themselves. Is your goal to be a better mom, wife, employee, artist, or boss? Or maybe you have a more basic physical goal of fitting into size 6 jeans. This isn't selfish and it isn't vain—it's about valuing yourself and your vi-sion! I bet if you take an in-depth look at that goal, you will find that your success in any of these roles is tied to your own health and personal happiness. Pause for a moment to consider the impact of your energy level, your health, and even your happiness on the life you want to lead. Sometimes a simple shift in perspective when it comes to goals is enough to see them through.

Do something for me:

- Take a moment to think and clear your mind.

- Enjoy this moment of calm and find joy in it!

- Now try to name one aspect of your body (or behavior)
  that you wish to change.

- Do you believe that this change is possible?

- Let's figure out a way to get you there!

These steps are a great way to get started with defining your goals. They don't take the energy of meditation or any other kind of mindfulness practice. In fact, their sim-plicity is what makes them so powerful: the goal that is right for you will be very clear to you if you take the time to slow down and listen to yourself. Of course, there is no one way to center your mind and get better connected with your body. Meditation and breathing exercises can be effective routes, but sometimes this connection can happen a lot more easily by simply taking a moment to balance, to pause and define what you really want. This sets you up for ongoing positive energy and thoughts.

Staying Focused and Letting the Community Support You

There are all sorts of situations that can derail us:

"I'm late! No time to get to the gym."

"I ate so badly last night and feel fat. I'll be 'good' today and work out again tomorrow."

"I am too tired to even think about making dinner."

"I cannot lose my baby weight."

So how do you stay focused on your goal when life gets in the way? You keep an open mind and use the mindset that prioritizes being flexible, trying new things, and staying connected to the program.

One of my newer clients, a mom in her late thirties, had not worked out since her early twenties. "All of a sudden," she found herself 15 pounds overweight and unable to either lose the weight or find time to exercise. "How do I get to a gym with a 16-month-old?" she asked me in quiet desperation.

In thinking rigidly about fitness and remembering her two-hour workouts at the gym and her course of diet and fitness as a type A undergraduate 15 years earlier, she couldn't understand how she would ever be able to mesh her two divergent lives. Was it possible to merge those two lives? Sure. Was it necessary? No! My advice was to forget the gym for now and let go of her guilt about it. I helped her begin putting a program together that involved a few exercises from my 15-minute Ballet Beautiful Blast Series and a longer 60-minute workout on days when she had the time. She was thrilled to see her body begin to tighten and tone again for the first time in years, putting in just a couple of days a week. These changes inspired her to begin eating better and setting bigger goals.

In order to stay connected to your ultimate goal—living Ballet Beautifully—you need to stay focused on the goal that's right in front of you. Many of the women doing

Ballet Beautiful use the community to help them stay focused; this connection to something larger than themselves also helps to reinforce their commitment to their goals. As Jenna remarked, "Everyone who does Ballet Beautiful has this great quality of understanding and accepting the emotional side of women, beauty, softness, while also being strong and opinionated."

Katherine spoke about "plugging into the Ballet Beautiful community and support system" as a way to "embrace our differences—women that come together to do Ballet Beautiful are from all different backgrounds, different body types. That's encouraging to me. It's a safety net—we are in the trenches together working hard to achieve our own individual goals and dreams."

As you will see in the upcoming pages, getting and staying connected to the Ballet Beautiful community will boost your confidence and your results! Sharing your Ballet Beautiful experience with others keeps you connected to your own goals and progress and tapped into the program in a way that is rewarding and fun.

The Simple Goal: Stay Away from Extremes and Work the Margins

To achieve even the loftiest of goals, you must employ a simple approach that comes down to steady, consistent work, every day. This is an important part of Ballet Beautiful. I'm not asking you to starve yourself, to consume only lemon juice and maple syrup for 10 days straight, or even to give up all dairy, sweets, coffee, and wine. But I am asking you to focus on yourself every day. That might be a 15-minute workout, or a 60-minute workout, or swapping out your nightly dessert for fresh fruit.

All you need to do is think about how you can take care of yourself, choose at least one thing to do from the program each day, and then focus on that.

Nicole shared how much Ballet Beautiful helped her gain balance in her nutrition. "I have always been very interested in nutrition, but there are a lot of mixed messages out there and it can get confusing. Doing Ballet Beautiful has enabled me to learn more about the importance of a healthy, balanced diet. Mary Helen's approach makes it so simple by emphasizing health and nutrition, which is the way that I now choose to live my life. I started not skipping breakfast even on mornings when I was busy or running late and eating more balanced whole foods. I wouldn't even consider going on a diet today. I'm thinner, more relaxed and I feel healthier too."

Take the time to make conscious choices until it doesn't feel like work anymore and is just a part of your new life.

Sample Goals

Whether your goal is to get into better shape for an upcoming event, go down a dress size, or simply shed extra weight that has been bothering you, it's important to think of that goal as being buoyed by your mindset, the food that you eat, how often and how long you work out, and the support you create to help keep you focused and committed.

For instance, if your goal is to lose one pound in one week, what foods can you take out of your diet? What foods will you replace them with? Removing processed foods and white refined sugar from your diet is a great way to start. Take those two items out and you will probably lose more than one pound a week. You'll also have more energy and better skin, and you'll start sleeping better too.

Some women choose not to focus on weight loss as a goal but rather find it more motivating to feel better; they might define their goal as Katherine did—to substitute the whole milk in her latte with skimmed milk.

Still other women frame their goal around exercise: they commit to doing 60 minutes of Ballet Beautiful Blasts three times a week.

What's amazing is that all these goals lead to the same results: a sleek, toned body that is much healthier and often a lot lighter.

Suzanne shared, "I wasn't sure what I was looking for when I started. Certainly my body had changed a bit after my first pregnancy. I was hoping to find something that counterbalanced those changes, but in a positive, fun, uplifting way. I also knew that I needed to feel strong and healthy as I went into my second pregnancy. Not only did all those things happen, but I love my body in its entirety now! I feel so confident and strong!"

Katherine's goal was to focus on the program itself and use its flexibility and accessibility to feel like she could attain her personal goals. "It's not a scary commitment. It's neatly organized, even though it's complex, which makes it easier to keep up with and a lot less intimidating."

Is your goal to lose weight? Eat better? Feel better? Tone your body? You don't need to name extreme goals to achieve your desired results. Keep the following in mind when you set your goals:

1. Be realistic about the time frame. You cannot lose 10 pounds overnight. Give yourself a couple of weeks and put a program in place that will help you lose in a healthy way and keep the weight off.

2. Think big but remember your pacing—small steps!

3. Come up with your plan: decide what areas of your body you want to work on and how you may (or may not) change your eating plan, and then create a schedule to execute this plan.

4. Envision the results—every day. This can be incredibly motivating and will empower your goal setting!

5. Remember to be flexible and prepared for the unexpected! This will prove invaluable in keeping you on track. Find ways to reward yourself that are in line with your goals and support them!

You don't need to overthink these steps; just keep it simple.

* * *

One thing I've learned from working with thousands of women around the world is that each individual is motivated in a singular way. You may be motivated to do Ballet Beautiful to elongate and tone your body and improve your posture. Your friend may be fixated on losing weight around her middle and having a healthier heart. Still another woman may be motivated to get her entire body one or two sizes smaller so she can wear shorts in the summer and feel confident.

Or your goal may have nothing to do with weight. You may feel sluggish and moody. You may have heard that "eating clean" can boost your energy and make you clearheaded. You may be already convinced that if you eat foods that are closer to nature, your body will respond intuitively. And it's true: whole foods make you feel lighter, think more clearly, and look your best and brightest.

As you move into the next chapter, you will bring together your mindset and your goals to make sure these are aligned for balance and success.

The more you work out, the stronger you feel. The stronger you feel, the more grounded you are. It's a positive feedback loop that keeps on giving.

The Perils of the Scale

To weigh or not to weigh—that is indeed a good question. I am of two minds on this topic. On the one hand, weighing yourself can help you stay attuned to your body and cue you into what can happen when you indulge in your favorite gelato one too many times or when you might even be losing too much weight. On the other hand, weighing yourself can become obsessive and lead to undereating . . . which in turn can lead to yo-yo dieting. Again, my approach is all about balance: using a scale can help you stay on track . . . if you don't overdo it. It's sort of like counting calories—it's a useful practice for some people and destructive for others. My advice is not to obsess over the number and to keep the focus on your health and happiness. If you need to put the scale away, you will be able to notice changes in your body—how your clothes fit, how you feel—without focusing too much on numbers.

So are you doing Ballet Beautiful to feel more confident?

Are you motivated by your own desires or the expectations of others?

My point here is to listen to *your* motivation. Stay in touch with *your* goal.

Revise, Re-envision, Reward Yourself

As you focus on your goals, know that as you get more into your Ballet Beautiful lifestyle, your goals will naturally shift. This is a good thing. You will accomplish one small goal and then want to set another for yourself. This may take two weeks or two months. The amount of time doesn't really matter. What matters is you.

- Revise your own goals as you progress

- Re-envision the end result

- Reward yourself along the way

Break the habit of using food as a reward for dieting! This is a negative cycle and closely tied to the overeating/undereating cycle. Find rewards for yourself that are not in conflict with your goals and embrace them! It could be taking a long soak in bath salts and indulging in an at-home spa evening in a face mask and your robe. Maybe it's a much-needed time-out from your life with a steaming pot of tea and your favorite novel, or a long walk when you get home from work. Rewards are important because they help you maintain your balance. Just remember, using food as a reward and looking forward to a large pizza and a pint of ice cream will not have the same effect!

In the next chapter, we will delve more into what it takes to create balance in your diet and in your life. Balance is a key to the Ballet Beautiful mindset that provides the foundation for flexibility in every way.

Chapter 3

Your Baseline

Achieving Balance and
Paying Attention to How You Feel

The life of a professional ballerina requires incredible physical strength, mental stability, and confidence—not only to stay committed to an art that makes such extreme physical demands, but to gather the pluck to perform onstage night after night in front of thousands of people.

The daily physical routine is brutal—it's no wonder that ballet dancers are famous for their discipline! When you spend more than 70 hours a week pushing your body to the max, in constant search of physical and artistic perfection, discipline is not optional. You live, think, dance, and even dream about ballet, almost by default, because you just don't have time for anything else. Days spent sewing and breaking in new shoes (sometimes as many as three or four pairs a day!), stretching, and rehearsing are punctuated by the bliss of an evening performance and the moment when your soul can really expand onstage. It's an unbelievably demanding lifestyle that takes a tremendous amount of dedication and focus, all of which hangs on a critical inner balance.

That is the tricky part. Finding balance in a world defined by extremes is really tough! I was counseled on multiple occasions to "put my blinders on," to "ignore everything and everyone around me," to focus only on dance. As an artist and as a woman, that wasn't the right formula for me. It made me feel caged in and stunted, like I couldn't grow or breathe. When I began living a rich life for myself outside of the theater, I realized that I needed to be more conscious about balance and began knitting together the important tasks of taking care of myself, eating right, and relaxing.

To achieve lasting success and happiness in anything you are doing, to stay grounded, focused, and confident, finding balance is a must. Without balance, you risk a burnout and all of its side effects.

Stay Away from Extremes

I was fortunate to learn early in my career that to take great care of my body I would have to train outside of the dance studio. I also learned (through considerable trial and error) that extremes in my diet led to unhappiness, insecurity, and physical instability. I may be a ballerina by training, but my body is made just like yours. I've gone through bouts of extreme dieting, to disastrous effect: I've learned the hard way that losing weight too fast ultimately backfires because you come to obsess over food and gain weight all over again in the end. This is not a healthy or productive way to live. In fact, it's incredibly frustrating and inefficient—for your metabolism, your mindset, and your body.

Finding balance in your diet and fitness routine will help you lose weight, look and feel better, and, most importantly, maintain those hard-earned results! While a quick fix can be incredibly seductive, I have learned that the true value of a fitness and lifestyle program is measured in how well it can be maintained. This means getting away from extremes (undereating or overeating, total lack of exercise or obsessive exercise) to stay focused and on track with your health and happiness. I cannot emphasize this enough! Just as I learned to balance my ballet classes, rehearsals, and performances with my Ballet Beautiful program and cross-training to keep my body strong and fit while dancing professionally, I have learned to achieve balance in my diet and my mind.

As Jenna described the program, "The Ballet Beautiful workouts are so portable and low-gear by nature, I find myself able to do a little bit when I'm just standing still. The workout becomes a more integrated way of movement, and a more constant part of my life—rather than me having to leave my life and go to the gym. I can really stay connected to myself and my identity even when I share the workout with others."

Balance is not simply about developing the strength and muscularity to perform the perfect grand jeté or triple pirouette. It's also about learning to stay grounded in yourself so that you know what you need, you keep your priorities in line, and at the same time you remain flexible and forgiving enough to not push yourself in counterproductive ways.

Balance also means staying in touch with how you feel. If you find yourself swinging from a lot of energy to a little, or waking up one morning feeling great and the next feeling glum, then you might be doing something else to trigger these mood shifts. Balance begins with the physical, but it's equal parts emotional and mental—you cannot have one without the other.

Your Body in Balance

To keep your body in balance, you must:

- Learn to listen

- Avoid deprivation

- Know when to move on if you have overindulged

- Always consider your body's needs

As we've talked about throughout the book, depriving your body leads to one thing: overeating and imbalance. Deprivation is never good for the body. Our bodies work best when they are receiving energy and nutrients from healthy whole foods. This could mean eating several small meals and snacks throughout the day or eating a healthy, balanced three meals a day. One good rule of thumb is to eat something healthy every four hours and try to avoid getting ravenous. (See the chapters in Part III for healthy snack and small meal suggestions!)

By eating regularly, you help your body maintain blood sugar, which wards off cravings that can get uncontrollable (for sugar and starchy carbs especially!) and keeps you feeling balanced. Going long stretches without eating will make your blood sugar drop and might leave you feeling light-headed, grouchy, and out of sorts. Often you will then eat too much once you do eat!

I think of deprivation as a dieting disaster, ruining your metabolism and setting you up for a nasty cycle of restricting and overeating. By now you should see these responses as red flags—extremes that threaten your balance, health, and success. In Chapter 8, I will share the specifics of planning and putting an eating plan into place, but for now I want you to focus on identifying and avoiding the triggers that lead to overeating—defined as emotional or thoughtless eating of extra calories that your mind never processes and your body doesn't need. This could be food you consume while driving, talking on the phone, standing in front of the fridge, or sitting in front of the TV. The best way to combat overeating is to take note that it's happening! You can't enjoy your food and find satisfaction if you don't even realize that you are consuming it.

Are You Undereating, Overeating, or Eating Just Enough?

One of the best ways to make changes in the margins and avoid extremes is to stay flexible in your mind. As you will see in the coming chapters, flexibility enables you to forgive yourself when you've had a bad day, stay focused on your *simple steps to goal achievement*, and figure out how to eat just enough.

Overeating and undereating are often a nasty cycle of imbalance, frustration, and emotional pain. In my own experience, I discovered a terrible causal relationship between the two: undereating often causes overeating, and vice versa. Ballet Beautiful is about celebrating your body and nurturing it to be its best, its strongest and most flexible; there is no room for that behavior here. Undereating is a punishment for your body when what it craves is the reward of proper nutrition. Undereating is also guaranteed to create wild cravings and throw your entire body and metabolism out of balance, potentially making you unhappy and overweight in the end.

Stay Active

Working out regularly is another important way to get into balance and stay there. Learning to listen to your body could mean noting whether you feel better working out in the mornings or the evenings—and then setting a program that works for you, satisfies you, and helps you achieve and maintain your goals. If you hate to work out in the morning, I am not going to tell you that is the best plan. Maybe for you it's best to work out in the evenings, when you can really let go of the stress of your day, focus on yourself, and enjoy yourself. But if work deadlines, family obligations, or invitations to happy hour always get in the way of your working out at night, I'm going to strongly suggest that you find a way to make exercise a part of your morning or mid-day routine.

One way to stay motivated is to listen to your body and pay attention to how good you feel when you do work out. This kind of attunement is a key to motivation. We all have worked out even when we didn't feel like it, knowing that it's going to make us feel so much better. Play this forward: when you feel sluggish, stressed, or time-constrained, remind yourself of this awesome cause-and-effect. Thinking about how great I'll feel after my workout always motivates me to push through!

Just as I don't skip meals, I always find at least 15 minutes each day to work out. Even when my day lasts 16 hours, rushing from meetings and training sessions, writing for my blog, and managing my growing Ballet Beautiful business, I find a little time to move, just for me. I know that I am lucky because I can often sneak in my own exercise when I am training or teaching class. But that doesn't happen every day; there are some days when I can't even put 15 minutes together to work out. I try to remember, however, the importance of balance and maintenance. So, on those days, I find myself doing a quick version of my Cardio Swan Arms at night while waiting for the pasta to boil, or some ab work before my shower in the morning. Remember: a little bit can go a long way—and every little piece counts!

Regular exercise has a very important domino effect: the more you exercise, the more your body gets accustomed to the physical activity, and the more the exercise invigorates you by speeding up your metabolism (so you're burning fat throughout the day!), the sharper your focus becomes and the longer your attention span. You can suddenly become more efficient, more confident, and suddenly more productive.

It doesn't take a professional training program with five hours a day or more of physical exercise to make this happen! Even when you are busy, if you make time for 10 or 15 minutes of exercise, you will feel better about yourself, make better food choices, and be more likely to work out again tomorrow.

Making Maintenance Work

When I look back at my early approach to dieting, I see clearly why I was destined to fail. My focus was on getting somewhere, but I had no clue how to maintain the results. Many lifelong dieters cringe when they hear the word *maintenance*. Why? Because it's a word that refers to the plateau that many people reach when they stick to a deprivation-based diet or it reminds them of past failures.

Ballet Beautiful is different. You are working hard to achieve your new Ballet Beautiful body, and maintaining it is simply about finding balance and staying away from the extremes. All you need to do is check in daily with yourself: What did I have for breakfast? Have I eaten enough fruits, veggies, and whole grains today? Should I do a 15-minute workout or a longer one? Have I had enough water today?

Such questions enable you to stay attuned to how you feel and what you need and help you develop the awareness and confidence either to stop eating before you get too full or to correct and adjust your eating habits when life gets hectic and you slip. This is the place where Ballet Beautiful becomes a part of your life, not just a new workout and diet program you are trying. It's the sweet spot, and I want to help you get there and stay there! It may not sound very sexy, but one of the keys to Ballet Beautiful's balanced approach is knowing that you can eat a slice or two of pizza and have a glass of wine with friends and still work out the next day with confidence and ease.

> ## Remember to Take a Rest Day
>
> I always take off one full day each week to rest, relax, and recover. The body needs the downtime, and the mind needs the break. But don't confuse a rest day with a cheat day! A rest day is about rewarding your body, but a cheat day is about eating like crazy and threatening the balance that makes Ballet Beautiful work.

Emotional Balance

All of us have reached for food to comfort ourselves, as a way to feel better when we are sad or simply having a bad day.

Imagine this scenario: You are stressed out and starving when you get home from work. Feeling anxious and on autopilot, you abandon your principle of balance and eat a huge meal followed by dessert. You wake up in the morning feeling bloated, lethargic, and generally upset. Yuck. Now you are experiencing more stress fueled by negative feelings about yourself and your body. What could possibly turn the day around? Skipping breakfast? No. When you go to your closet and look at your skinny jeans, you feel suddenly miserable, convinced that you will never fit in them today. You feel hopeless, you're angry with yourself, and suddenly you're dreaming about how great chocolate ice cream would taste right now . . . it's too late for you this week anyhow, right?

Wrong! I have given in to feelings of self-doubt, even self-loathing, and stood in front of the freezer eating that chocolate ice cream for breakfast. It didn't make me look or feel very good. I am, however, incredibly happy to say that I learned to identify the problem and correct it, and you can too. I don't deny myself chocolate ice cream when I really want it; I just ignore the craving before lunch!

When I was in the throes of a moment like this one, I felt totally out of control. I didn't know that what I really needed to turn my day around was to leave the skinny jeans in the closet and pick a different outfit, eat something healthy and wholesome like a slice of whole-grain bread with fresh avocado, and move on. I also didn't realize that what I needed most was to be forgiving and kind in how I treated myself, rather than frustrated, angry, and sad. Talk about silencing those nasty negative voices! When you feel backed into a corner, take a minute to reframe your choices.

How did I learn this? Trial and error. In the big picture, chocolate ice cream for breakfast is probably no worse than pancakes or waffles on occasion, but I found that instead of making me feel better, giving in to emotional eating made me feel worse.

Emotional eating is a huge problem for so many of us—but one that we can overcome! In the world of dance, it was easy to absorb and mimic the bad habits of others, and it was also hard to let those habits go. In developing my own program, I started paying better attention to my own patterns of emotional eating. I learned to identify my triggers for emotional or thoughtless eating so that I could consciously avoid certain situations and realign myself. I work to pay attention to these triggers to this day.

Let's back up a minute. If you have woken up feeling puffy and lethargic, take a moment to recognize these as physical qualities. Perhaps you feel bloated because you have PMS, or because you drank two glasses of wine the night before and had too many olives before dinner or an overly salty meal. Bloatedness can even come from eating a high-fiber meal before dinner when your body isn't used to it. It can be hard not to feel bad about your body and yourself when you feel like this. But there is always a physical reason behind bloating and lethargy. It could be cabbage that makes you feel bloated! The point is that it doesn't have to be bad things that make you feel bloated—it might be the high-fiber toast or fresh mango slices you had for breakfast!

Now, take a moment to follow the trail: if your body feels bloated, how does that make you feel *emotionally?* Maybe the bloating makes you feel guilty, ashamed, embarrassed, sad, or just plain bad about yourself. These negative feelings are more than likely left over from your other experiences with food. It's so common for women (and men!) to turn to food when they are uncomfortable with their feelings. This can begin early in life—perhaps your mother gave you a bottle as soon as you fussed, or cookies when you cried. Your family culture may have been one that turned to food not only in celebration but also in times of stress or crisis. While eating food is a natural, purely human response, the danger comes when you eat too much because your eating is prompted by emotions (especially negative ones!) rather than your body's natural cycle of hunger. This is the cycle we want to—and can—break.

Are You Really Hungry?

The next time you find yourself thinking about or reaching for your comfort foods, take these two steps:

1. Take a deep breath and let it out.

2. Then ask yourself if you are feeling physical hunger or if you are just tired, thirsty, or upset.

If you take the time to become aware of whether what you are feeling is actual hunger or another feeling that is emotional in nature, then you give yourself the opportunity to break an unconscious habit of eating emotionally. These two steps may seem oversimplistic, but I assure you that they work. They can also help you make better choices about the food you eat when you are feeling emotionally overwhelmed and help you regain your inner balance. Why? Because all of us have the power to become aware of how we are feeling and to choose not to let that have an impact on how we eat.

You can also learn to indulge your cravings in a balanced, moderate way. I have found moderate indulging in some of my favorite foods, foods that once might have been considered forbidden, is one of the greatest things I can do to keep my body in balance. I eat chocolate every day! I indulge in a little bit of cheese and wine before dinner most nights and don't set a lot of "off-limits" rules about food. But I also pay attention to how these favorite foods make me feel. If I'm starving before dinner, I try to start by eating raw veggies and hummus and a few olives before I dive into the cheese (goat's cheese, not triple cream Brie!). Then, when I have a small bite of the cheese, I really savor it! I take the time to slow down and enjoy the experience of eating. This helps me stay in touch with how I feel and lets me feel satisfied with less. On weeknights when I am training early the next morning, I usually don't finish my glass of wine. But on a weekend I allow myself an extra drink if I feel the need.

I also don't skip meals, no matter how busy I am or how late I am running. I always grab a snack and often bring it with me so that I don't find myself stuck somewhere—either without food or with the only choice being a chocolate bar! You know it as well as I do: skipping meals leads to poor food choices.

As you will see in Chapter 8, one of the best ways to stay in balance is to eat frequently—I eat probably two or three snacks a day and three to four small meals a day. That may sound like a lot, but if you are choosing foods that your body needs and uses, then eating often helps your body burn calories and keeps your blood sugar stable.

Pay Attention to How You Feel

As I made the transition from the rigors of dancing with a ballet company to founding and becoming CEO of Ballet Beautiful, I had to learn a powerful lesson: how to take care of myself. The foundation of taking care of myself, I realized, was paying attention to how my body felt. When I was pushing through my pain, not admitting to myself that my foot was injured, I was unwittingly undermining my own recovery.

Over time I began to do regular check-ins, asking myself questions and letting my body communicate with me:

- Is that a sore muscle or a tender joint?

- Did that snack make me feel good and grounded or slightly off?

- Why do I feel groggy?

- What did I eat that makes me feel so good today?

I realized that by zeroing in on what hurt, what made me feel strong, what felt tight, or what felt weak, I could then tailor my workouts even more specifically.

Once you pinpoint how your body feels and begin to listen to your body with new awareness, you will be able to make connections between what you are doing (eating, exercising, and so on) and how you are feeling. You can then use this insight to self-monitor and adjust your workouts. As you will soon see, there are many options for workouts—single workouts, combined workouts, short workouts, and long workouts—and several areas of the body to target during your workouts. The more aware and attuned to yourself you are, the better able you'll be to design a specific workout for any given day or week and the more engaged you'll be in it. And enhancing your engagement will not only reinforce your commitment but help you achieve your Ballet Beautiful goals!

Here is a quick checklist you can use to isolate how you feel:

1. Are you energized?

2. Do you feel fatigued?

3. Do you feel irritable or grouchy?

4. Are you generally happy and content?

Once you've pinpointed how you feel, take a step back and think about your day: Do you feel good about what you ate? Did you treat your body well with a healthy breakfast and fresh, whole foods throughout the day? How does this make you feel physically? If you ate a lot of unhealthy or processed foods, what's the correlation to your emotional state? Did you move your body? How did that make you feel? Stepping back a couple of times a day and really taking the time to focus on how you feel will help you find the elements in your day that contribute to your well-being.

One important lesson I've learned is that it's possible to learn to truly like healthy foods and exercise. Many of the women I work with have been shocked at not only how good they feel once they change their eating habits, but how good real food actually tastes. Begin by paying attention to the way certain foods make you feel. If you are feeling good after you eat something, it's probably good for you. If you feel heavy, sleepy, or bad about yourself, the reason could be the high starch or sugar content or the additives and chemicals (yes, the chemicals in processed foods do have physiological effects!) of food you're eating that is unhealthy or perhaps best enjoyed in moderation. You can learn to enjoy indulging in such food, savoring each bite, but then move on!

Mental Balance: The Key to Your Baseline

Physical and emotional balance are closely intertwined, and both kinds of balance begin by eating well and often, making healthy food choices, and paying attention to how you feel. When these habits are in place, you give yourself the opportunity to maintain mental balance, defined as thinking clearly, staying focused, and following through on your goals (whether a daily, a two-month, or a lifelong goal).

Mental balance is the key to your baseline—that sense of being connected to the inner you, grounded in real feelings, centered in yourself, and confident as you approach each and every day. When you build mental balance, you are better able to manage challenges, withstand setbacks, and keep charging ahead.

Ballet Beautiful Balance Checklist

Let's do a quick review of how to make sure you're living in balance:

1. *Are you taking care of your body?* Make sure you work out at least three days a week, with five or six days being optimal. A workout can be as brief as one

15-minute Body Blast or as challenging as a 60-minute Classic. Or it can be a well-targeted hybrid workout focused on arms and legs, combining two 15-minute segments.

2. *Are you keeping your emotional eating in check?* Are you developing awareness of your habits? Are you making sure you're really hungry when you reach for a snack? Are you pausing to tune in to any uncomfortable feeling that may be triggering a craving?

3. *Are you regularly rewarding yourself?* As you've learned in this chapter, becoming familiar with the difference between hunger and anxiety, stress, or fear enables you to choose doing something nice for yourself as a reward instead of drowning your feelings in jellybeans. Non-food-related ways to treat yourself and stay on track include buying a magazine and nail polish, treating yourself to an at-home spa experience, giving yourself a few minutes to browse your favorite e-shopping site, or even taking a power nap!

4. *Are you eating right?* Remember to eat often and to choose healthy foods.

5. *How positive and healthy is your thought process?* (Especially when thinking about yourself!)

When you eat well and work out at least 15 minutes, six days a week, your body will thank you. And you will realize that you can indeed maintain balance.

As you learn to pay attention to how you feel and to root out patterns that are not aligned with your health and fitness goals, you will naturally and easily fall into balance—physically, emotionally, and mentally. Keep in mind that we all eat emotionally—it's natural to seek comfort in food when we feel bad, uncomfortable, or sad, or have any other feeling that upsets our inner homeostasis. With a heightened awareness of when you're at risk of emotional eating, you can avoid derailing a day of healthy eating and exercise with one too many bites of a cupcake, triggering uncontrollable cravings by having too many cocktails, or putting yourself in a funk after you couldn't stop eating an entire pint of Häagen-Dazs instead of switching to a lighter dessert.

Being in balance is the essence of living the Ballet Beautiful mindset. As you become aware of your inner attitudes and shift from a negative attitude to one that is positive and growth-oriented, you will have an easier time identifying and setting realistic, self-empowering goals. With this clarity, you will naturally tap into your own motivation for achieving your goals, making you feel ever more confident and strong. These building blocks are the foundation for achieving the physical, emotional, and mental balance that secures your baseline. From here the only way is up!

PART II

THE BALLET BEAUTIFUL PROGRAM

*I want every woman to feel the power
of grace, strength, and possibility!*

Chapter 4

The Ballet Beautiful Method

The Basics

Some people will tell you that you have to be a professional ballerina to look like one. And others will say that you can't actually target and transform specific parts of your body . . . that if you want to have leaner hips or a flatter stomach you have to work out your entire body. I couldn't disagree more.

I believe that every woman has the ability to transform her body. I have seen my Ballet Beautiful method dramatically change the bodies and lives of countless women all over the world, including my own, and I know that it can do the same for you. In this part of the book, you will learn how to tune in to where your ballet muscles are and, more importantly, how you can begin to sculpt and reshape the way your body looks and moves. We are going to break down the basics of the Ballet Beautiful method together as I explain how this program targets and exhausts the key "ballet muscles" through low-impact exercises and stretches designed to give anyone the graceful lines, fluid movement, and beautiful posture of a ballet dancer. This is what makes Ballet Beautiful different from other programs: it's the secret behind my method and your incredible results.

To keep it simple, I focus on five features of your Ballet Beautiful body:

1. *Flexibility:* Everyone can increase flexibility and become more agile through daily stretching. Each Ballet Beautiful workout begins and ends with a good stretch to keep the muscles long and limber!

2. *Strong center:* A ballerina's strength, posture, and grace all extend from a strong but narrow center. The Ballet Beautiful exercises target the muscles deep in the abdominals, center, and back that are key to building a dancer's strong center of balance!

3. *Great butt:* Ballet dancers are known for their tight, toned butts! My exercises tighten, tone, and lift the butt. If you already have a great butt and are concerned about exercising it away, don't worry—that won't happen with Ballet Beautiful!

4. *Long, toned legs:* Ballerinas have incredibly powerful legs with long, lean muscles. Ballet Beautiful sculpts and defines the elongated muscles that are key to powerful legs.

5. *Lean, feminine arms and elegant posture:* Ballet dancers have strong yet elegant upper bodies! My Upper Body Series improves posture, strengthens the center, and sculpts a toned yet graceful upper body.

Your Ballet Muscles

Ballet dancers have a body shape, carriage, and way of moving that is one of a kind. The reason is simple: ballet training targets and uses muscles that are not used in other fitness programs or sports. The body shape, posture, and movement that result from this training are as unique as the training itself. That may sound intimidating, but almost anyone can get used to it. I myself never loved the idea of pointe shoes, but they have become like a second skin to me! So here is the good news: through Ballet Beautiful, you will wake up and engage your "ballet muscles" (everybody has them!) as you build the elegant body shape of a dancer, develop beautiful posture, and increase your flexibility. Together we will use a simple series of targeted, ballet-inspired exercises and stretches that focus on creating this specific form and posture. The aesthetic is graceful and feminine, balanced by power and strength.

Your Ballet Primer: A Quick Look at Ballet Terms

Ballet was born in the courts of France, so most of the positions and movements are still expressed in French. Of course, you don't need to be able to speak French in order to understand how to do the movements, but as you become accustomed to the Ballet Beautiful workout, it might be helpful to refer to this brief guide. And you may find that sometimes the French terms—their direct translations—will help you visualize a movement.

Alignment: The lining up of parts of your body to make a balanced and graceful line.

Arabesque [a-ra-BESK]: A classic ballet position with one leg stretched long behind the dancer on the floor or in the air and the back knee straight. The supporting leg can be straight or bent into a demi-plié. The positions of the arms and hips determine whether the dancer is in first, second, third, or fourth arabesque.

Assemblé [a-sahm-BLAY]: Assembled or joined together. A step in which the working foot slides along the ground, brushing up into the air to bring both feet and legs together.

Attitude [a-tee-TEWD]: A position in which one leg is raised with the knee bent at a right angle and higher than the foot. The supporting leg can be straight, on pointe, or on demi-pointe, and the leg lifted in attitude can be to the front (as in attitude front), side, or back.

Battement [bat-MAHN]: The beating of the working leg.

Coupé [koo-PAY]: In this movement, from the French "to cut," one foot is lifted off the floor and "cuts" either in front of or behind the other. The toes of the working foot lift and point by the ankle of the supporting leg.

Extension [eks-tahn-SYAWN]: Extension of the limbs in the air; the ability to lift and hold the legs in the air.

Fondu, or fondue [fawn-DEW]: Sinking down. A term used to describe the bending and stretching of the standing knee.

Passé [pa-say]: A movement in which the working leg lifts and passes along the supporting leg by the knee.

Pirouette [peer-WET]: A turn on one leg.

Plié [plee-AY]: Bent, bending. A plié is a bend of the knees. A full bending of the knees is a *grand plié* and a *demi-plié* is a half-bending of the knees. The bending movement should be gradual and smooth, as should the rising movement. In a demi-plié the heels do not lift from the ground.

Pointe shoes: The satin shoes that allow ballerinas to dance on their toes.

Port de bras [pawr duh brah]: Carriage of the arms. The graceful movement or passage of the arms from one position to another.

Relevé [ruhl-VAY]: Raised. A raising of the body on the ball of the foot or on demi-pointe.

Rond de jambe [rawn duh zhahmb]: "Round" of the leg. A circular movement of the leg, on the ground or in the air.

Rond de jambe en l'air [rawn duh zhahmb ahn lehr]: A raised circular movement of the leg in the air.

Supporting leg: The supporting or standing leg is the one that holds the most weight in any movement or position.

Tendu [tan-doo]: Tight or stretched. Tendu is a common abbreviation for *battement tendu,* when the working leg is extended—to either the front, side, or back—along the floor until only the tip of the toe remains touching the floor. A tendu can also be used in preparation for more complex steps, such as pirouettes or leaps.

Turnout: The degree to which a dancer opens or turns out her feet and legs from the hip joints in any one position.

Working leg: The leg that is executing a given movement while the weight of the body is on the supporting leg.

Ballet Positions

In ballet there are five basic positions for the feet and arms. Almost every basic movement in ballet begins and ends in one of these positions.

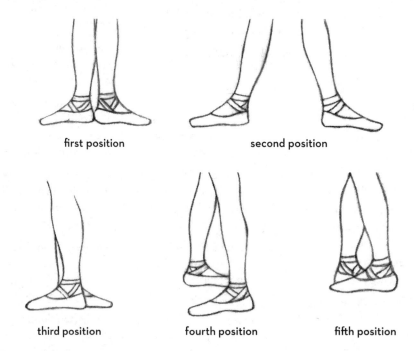

first position   second position

third position   fourth position   fifth position

Positions of the Ballet Feet

- *First position:* The toes are turned out and the heels touch each other.

- *Second position:* The heels are separated about hip width apart and the feet remain in turnout.

- *Third position:* One foot is in front of the other, with the back of the front heel touching the middle of the back foot.

- *Fourth position:* One foot is in front of the other, with the front heel positioned about one step from the back foot, but angled toward the middle, as in third position.

- *Fifth position:* Both feet come together, with the toes of each foot meeting the heels of the other.

- *Sixth position:* Both feet are together, touching at the heels and the toes. *Note:* Sixth position is an add on with both feet in parallel that I sometimes use in my standing blasts.

first position

second position

third position

fourth position

fifth position

Positions of the Ballet Arms

- *First position:* Arms are extended to the front in a circle, with the hands in line with the waist.

- *Second position:* Arms are open wide to the sides, with the elbows slightly round and lifted.

- *Third position:* One arm rounds in front (as in first position), and the other arm extends out to the side (as in second position).

- *Fourth position:* One arm rounds in front, and the other extends above the head—again, rounded at the elbow, fingers relaxed.

- *Fifth position:* Both arms are lifted up over the head and rounded into a circle (similar to first position).

When doing an arabesque, the position of the feet changes based on the placement of the arms and hips. See our guide on the following page!

first arabesque

second arabesque

third arabesque

Basic Arabesque Positions

- *First arabesque:* Beginning in an arabesque position (one leg stretched out long behind you on the floor, the supporting leg straight), extend the same arm as the working leg out to second position. Extend the other arm (same arm as the standing leg) to the front with the hand at shoulder height.

- *Second arabesque:* Begin in an arabesque position. Extend the working side arm across the body and out to the front and the standing side arm to second position.

- *Third arabesque:* Begin in an arabesque position. Extend both arms forward with the elbows straight. The working arm should be at shoulder height, as in first arabesque, and slightly lower than the standing arm, with about 16 inches between the hands.

The Ballet Beautiful
Approach to Stretching

Stretching, a huge part of a dancer's daily life, keeps muscles loose and the body limber. Dancers are always working to be more fluid and agile—we stretch at the beginning, middle, and end of any dance class, rehearsal, and, yes, even a workout! As you will see in the workout chapters, I encourage you to stretch before you begin exercising, whether your workout is for 15, 30, or 60 minutes. I also suggest that you stretch and release your muscles between movements. You will find that, as the muscles you are working become fatigued during a workout, it's important to stop, take a quick sip of water, and stretch out these muscles to keep them long and lean. If you are a beginner and just getting started with the program, taking extra time to stretch between exercises and performing fewer reps will also help you to modify your workout, giving your body a chance to rest as you build strength over time.

One of the key reasons I remind you to stop and stretch in between movements throughout the Ballet Beautiful workout is to keep your body as fluid and warm as possible. Can the exercises and stretches in Ballet Beautiful help you gain flexibility and improve your movement? Absolutely. If you are feeling stiff and achy, that's just your body's way of asking you to move. Gentle stretches and the Ballet Beautiful exercises will make an incredible difference in how you look and feel and how your body moves. The program keeps joints strong yet mobile and muscles taut but long. While I'm not promising extreme flexibility and an immediate center split, I can promise that daily stretching will increase your flexibility over time and help relieve stiff, achy joints. If you spend a lot of time driving, sitting, or hunched over a computer, these stretches can also lessen back pain and keep you limber.

I look at daily stretching as a necessary luxury and an important part of my beauty routine. It keeps my muscles released and gives me a chance to relax, focus on my body, and just enjoy the moment. When I was performing with the New York City Ballet, setting aside some quiet time to stretch before warming up always helped me prepare my body for the stage and calm and center my mind. After finishing my hair and makeup, I would pack on the layers of legwarmers, dance sweaters, and a huge fleecy sweatshirt with a zipper (easy to remove without disturbing my hair and makeup!) and head backstage to find a quiet corner to stretch out before the show. Because my muscles are used to being constantly stretched, I find that they crave it every day. Stretching is like a healthy addiction—my body always wants more!

My approach to stretching is different than many other exercise programs. Instead of thinking of stretching as an add-on, as something to do before or after a workout, I think of stretching as necessary and ongoing throughout the workout. Stretching helps release and lengthen muscles as you strengthen and tone them and plays an important role in your recovery after a workout. Remember that the ballet term "tendu" means "stretched" or "pulled"? Keep that in mind as you go: many of the instructions for my exercises will urge you to extend and stretch long through your limbs for the best results.

The Basic Stretches

Here are the basic stretches you will use throughout the BB workouts, whether you are doing the 60-Minute Classic or one of the four 15-Minute Blasts. Hold stretches for anywhere from 10 to 90 seconds, depending on how much time you have available and how tight your body feels.

The Classic Hamstring Stretch

a Sit on the floor, with your legs in front of you. Bend one knee in and stretch the other leg out long in front.

b Lean your upper body up and over the extended leg with the goal of reaching toward your foot. If you cannot reach your foot at first, just focus on reaching in that direction, moving your hands down your leg and shin as you gain flexibility.

c Exhale and extend forward, further down into the stretch, as you let your opposite hip drop down toward the floor.

d Don't worry about whether or not your hip reaches the floor or how low it is; everyone's hips are different. Your hips will loosen and open over time.

e For a more advanced variation, add a twist in the upper body. While extending forward with the upper body, lift the arm on the same side as your extended leg into the air, looking up and back behind you and taking a gentle twist with the spine. Open through the chest and stretch long through the arms.

f Repeat on the other side.

Hip Opener (Loose Pigeon)

This hip opener works miracles, but be patient and gentle as your body loosens.

a Begin seated on the mat. Bend your front knee in toward your hip and stretch your back knee out long behind you.

b Sit up high and open through the chest, pulling your stomach in.

c Gently bend toward the bent knee for a stretch through the spine. As with the first stretch, don't worry about whether or not your hip reaches the floor or how low it is— your hips will loosen and open over time.

d Repeat on the other side.

Inner Thigh Stretch

a Begin seated on the mat. Extend one leg out to the side as if preparing for a center split and reach toward your foot. Bend the other leg into a passé position, slightly to the front.

b Stretch the knee of the extended leg and lift your opposite arm up into a port de bras, curved above your head, reaching up and over toward the extended leg and stretching through the upper body. Curve your other arm low in front of you.

c Release through the side and back.

d Repeat on the other side.

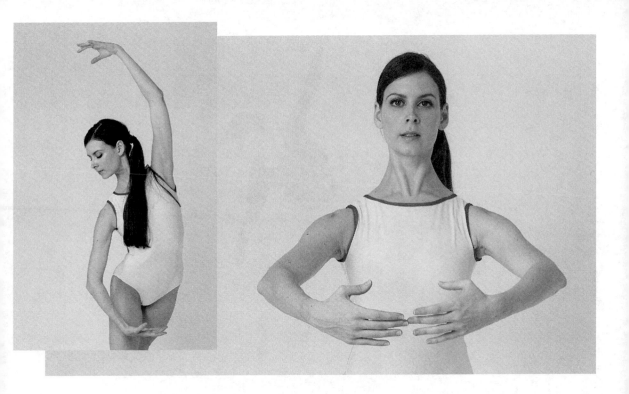

Upper Body Stretch
with Port de Bras

a This stretch can be done sitting or
   standing. Lift both of your arms up high to
   fifth position (in a circle over your head),
   staying relaxed through your neck and
   shoulders.

b Drop one arm down to fourth position
   (curved in front of you, low, at your hips),
   pulling your stomach in and connecting
   to your center. Take a breath in and then
   lift up and over, with the top arm
   extending out.

c Bring both arms down through first
   position (curved in a circle in front of you),
   then lift both arms back high to fifth
   position with the arms.

d Repeat the stretch on the other side.

Standing Stretch for Legs

This is a great stretch for the Blast Series work, as well as a terrific way to release your muscles at the office or even between classes at school!

a Bend your right leg in and grab the top of your foot with your right hand, pulling the foot up toward the butt, opening up through the front of the hip and thigh. For balance, pull in through your center or hold on to a wall or chair.

b Change legs and repeat.

c Extend your right leg in front and bend your body forward over that leg in a tendu (foot pointed and stretched out in front of you), keeping the knee straight. Pulse and release through the back of the leg and hamstring. Come up and change legs.

Stretching doesn't have to be technical, so don't obsess over your form, which will vary from day to day based on how tight you are and what you have been doing with your body. Be certain that you work within your range of motion and that the release of your muscles feels great as you go.

Now here are three variations on my basic Ballet Beautiful stretches. Feel free to weave them into your workout!

Seated Hamstring Stretch

I love this variation on the Classic Hamstring Stretch. I mix this in during the Classic Workout when I am already on my mat or as part of my cool down after one of the Blasts.

a Begin seated on your mat with both legs extended out long in front of you. Lift one leg up into the air and pull it towards your chest, keeping the knee straight. If you are very flexible, you can place your hands on your foot; if your muscles are tighter, get started by placing your hands on the calf of the extended leg or even behind the knee.

b Work within your range of motion as the back of the leg and hamstring begins to stretch out and release. Start at 90 degrees and then bring your leg back further toward your chest if possible.

c For a more advanced version and a deeper stretch try this exact movement lying on your back.

Center Splits

The center split is a terrific inner thigh stretch and a great way to increase flexibility through the insides and backs of your legs and hips. You don't need to worry about opening the legs to 180 degrees. Begin slowly and your splits will open in time.

a Begin seated on the floor with both legs extended to the side, keeping the knees straight.

b Place your hands on the floor between your legs and scoot your hips forward, opening your legs to the side as you go.

c Keep your upper body upright and your stomach pulled in. When your legs have opened as far as they will go, you can rock your hips forward for a deeper inner thigh stretch.

Seated Hip Opener

This exercise is a gentle hip opener that you can use throughout the Classic Workout and seated exercises. It's one of my favorites for the warm-up and cool-down because it is very gentle yet effective.

a Begin seated on the mat. Bend your right knee in toward your right hip on the mat. Lift your left knee and cross your left leg over your right leg, keeping the right foot on the ground.

b Keep your upper body lifted and your stomach in.

c Pull your left knee back toward your chest with your right hand for a deeper stretch through the back of the leg and hip.

d /A. For a more advanced version of this stretch, lift your left foot and leg into the air, bending your knee in the air in an attitude front.

e Using both arms, pull your knee back toward your chest and balance on your hips.

f Repeat on the other side.

Proper Ballet Beautiful Form

Perfect ballet technique begins with the basics, and the same is true for getting great results from the Ballet Beautiful method: having the right form is everything! As you go through the movements, it's very important to keep your body in proper alignment. The same exercise can give you very different results if your placement and form are incorrect, so I want to take the time with you now to get it right. Let's begin by getting into a really great resting position, a neutral position to which you can continually return and use to remind yourself of your Ballet Beautiful program, whether you are sitting in your car, working at your desk, or standing in line at the grocery store!

Your ideal resting position is one that is strong yet lifted, with your chin lifted, your neck relaxed, and your shoulders down. This position is the base for building great posture, and it is key to your Ballet Beautiful form. Whether you are sitting or standing, your posture should be regal and erect—it should inspire confidence in yourself, and when it does, I know that it will do the same in others. Proper form isn't reserved just for our workouts—try it in your next meeting or interview and see how you feel. I always find that I feel more confident and powerful when I stand or sit upright. (See the box on page 64 for a quick posture-check you can do anytime!)

Many of our lives are incredibly stressful, requiring constant juggling to get it all done. We carry heavy bags on our shoulders, wear weighted backpacks that weaken our lower back muscles, or perch kids on our hip, throwing it out of whack. This physical pressure combined with an increasingly sedentary lifestyle can affect our overall alignment and posture. All of us, however, need to be conscious of our alignment. How much time a

A Word About Flexibility

Many people, especially those who say they are not flexible, believe that some people are born able to bend and others are born without this ability. True? Sort of. We all have a different range of motion, and there is no question that some people are hypermobile. I happen to have very open joints and hips and legs that in many ways were built for ballet. But in the same way that you can target and tone your inner thighs, you can increase your flexibility and improve your range of motion. So whether your goal is to simply be able to reach your toes or to achieve the perfect center split, I will help you work to achieve it. And increasing flexibility over time changes and improves how your body feels and moves.

day do you spend bent over a computer at your desk or in a car hunched over the steering wheel? The more time you spend sitting down, the more likely your frame is to crumple or slump, weakening your center and wreaking havoc on your back.

Just writing about this is making me feel antsy! I'm going to stand up and take time for a quick stretch and stroll and put into practice my own tips on how to quickly reconnect with my elegant ballet posture before we move on. Try it with me:

- Stand up very tall and straight, extending through your vertebrae and spine.

- Pull your stomach in tight, stretch through the front of your hips and legs, and extend long through your joints.

This exercise should leave your body feeling stretchy, elongated, and energized. There is a push-and-pull to this too—you are lifting and stretching through your center and your limbs as you push your shoulders down, keeping your neck long.

Perfect Posture

Upright carriage and elegant posture are a ballet dancer's calling card. Ballerinas spend hours every day performing incredibly difficult steps and movements in a perfectly upright position. This action engages muscles through the center, the back, and all across the upper body that strengthen and develop excellent posture. The upper body work in my exercises mimics this process, helping you build the strength you need to experience and maintain perfect ballet posture from home! It's also the foundation for great Ballet Beautiful form, as I explain on page 64.

Workout Space and Equipment

I recommend choosing a space for your Ballet Beautiful workout that is quiet, calm, and uncluttered, with room for a towel or a mat. This is going to mean different things for different people, so just focus on finding an area that lets you focus on yourself.

POSTURE-CHECKS

Getting in the habit of spot-checking your posture throughout your day will help you improve it. When you feel hunched over, stiff, or achy, take a moment to straighten up your spine. It will change the way your body feels and give you clarity of mind!

Try doing this exercise throughout the day:

a Pull your stomach in and open your chest.

b Take a deep breath and imagine that you are carrying a stack of books on your head.

c Lift your arms out to the side in second position, stretching all the way through to your fingertips. Keep your neck long and your stomach pulled in tight.

d Imagine that someone is lightly touching you between your shoulder blades and open your chest without arching your back.

e Keep your stomach engaged.

f Now drop your hands to your sides, but don't relax your center or your spine.

This is how to get Ballet Beautiful posture in an instant!

The only equipment you'll need—if you can call it that—is a mat (or a towel if you're traveling). That's it! You do not need a barre, a pair of pointe shoes, a dance studio, or weights. You can do a Ballet Beautiful workout in the comfort of your own home or in a hotel room when you travel. I even have clients who do Ballet Beautiful in their office on busy days! If you already attend a gym, you can find a mat section of your gym or an empty corner to lay down a mat or towel and do a quick Ballet Beautiful workout while you're there. Just don't be surprised if people ask you if you are a ballerina when they see you stretching and practicing a set of Ballet Beautiful pliés and lunges!

Some of my clients ask whether they need to do the workout in front of a mirror. This is entirely a question of personal preference. The mirror played a big role in my life during the years I spent dancing with the New York City Ballet, and I am happy to take a break from it now. During my years with the company, I would start my day in the morning with a cup of coffee, sewing pointe shoes in front of the mirror at my dressing table, and then spend all day dancing in front of a mirror in class and rehearsals. Downtime for meals or resting my feet at my dressing table left me staring at my reflection even if I was not pulling my hair into the perfect bun for the stage or putting my makeup on. The physical therapy room was filled with mirrors too—the only escape from mirrors was onstage at night. I will take the cool inky black expanse of a full audience over my own reflection any day! This is probably why I enjoy practicing Ballet Beautiful without a mirror now—I can focus on how I feel rather than how I look.

Workout Clothes

I have spent years dancing and working out in a leotard and love the comfort and ease of wearing one when I work out. I also enjoy wearing a pair of my ballet slippers because they make me feel graceful and elegant! They also provide a great grip on some of the mat work and allow you to slide your feet with ease in the standing Blasts. This gear may help you really get into a particular mood or mindset. But bare feet or socks will also do. Ballet Beautiful is a flexible program, and that holds true for your outfit—you can wear whatever you wish and whatever enables you to move with confidence and ease. I do, however, recommend wearing form-fitting pants that let you see the lines of your legs so that you can track when your knees are truly bent or straight, for better form.

Hydration

I suggest sipping water throughout your workout. We all have heard that it is important to drink eight glasses of water a day and to stay hydrated; this is such common advice that many of us may even forget why water is so necessary for our health—especially when working out.

Water keeps your muscles fluid instead of tight and allows oxygen to flow through your body as you work out. Water's many other functions include boosting metabolism, flushing toxins, and regulating your body temperature.

Your body loses water as you exercise, so the harder you work out, the more you need to replace the fluids. It's much healthier for you to sip as you go rather than deprive your body of water during an intense workout. This may be obvious to you, but it wasn't to me, so I want to take a moment to expand!

When I started dancing with the New York City Ballet, I was only 16 and I didn't receive a lot of guidance on how to take care of my body. I wasn't in the habit of drinking a lot of water because it wasn't something that I did as a kid taking ballet in Charlotte. And when I suddenly found myself performing and dancing 70 hours a week, I didn't know how much water my body needed. I experienced a period of terrible fatigue that was a total mystery to me. I can clearly remember being exhausted constantly and thinking it had to be something in my diet, that I wasn't eating enough protein or carbs or vegetables. . . .

One Saturday afternoon I was feeling particularly bad after taking class in the morning and dancing three ballets in the matinee. When I casually mentioned that I had only had a coffee to drink that day, one of the older girls in the dressing room explained to me that I was probably deeply dehydrated (I was!) and that I should start drinking way more immediately. I bought and drank a big bottle of water, and from that day on I tried to make drinking water a regular part of my routine. When I made this simple change, I cannot tell

Hydrate with Ballet Beautiful

There are numerous benefits to staying hydrated! Here are some of my favorites:

1. Helps weight loss by regulating your appetite (sometimes we eat when our bodies are thirsty!)

2. Keeps skin dewy and fresh

3. Aids in digestion

4. Relieves fatigue

If you don't like the taste of water, try adding in fresh fruit or lemon slices. Start paying attention to how much better your body feels. You'll forget that water is "boring" when it makes you feel that great! Remember, if you're thirsty, you're already dehydrated, so be sure to keep water with you at all times—and drink up!

you how much better my body felt. My fatigue lessened, and my energy increased dramatically. It was a lesson I'll never forget.

I find that one of the best ways to stay hydrated is to keep a water bottle with you at all times. You don't have to spend money on exotic mineral waters that promise better filtration or purity. But you might want to think about investing in a water filtration system so you can refill your bottle from home and sip it throughout the day.

The Ballet Beautiful Principles

Before we get started, here's a reminder of the Ballet Beautiful principles:

1
Connect with Your Center

Ballet dancers have incredibly strong centers because we are constantly pulling in and engaging our abdominals. This action can change the simplest step, exercise, or even resting position into a great ab workout. This doesn't just mean sucking in your breath to try to flatten your stomach. Connecting to your center is about pulling in your lower abs, the place between your hip bones and underneath your belly button. It's what happens naturally when you laugh or gasp with surprise.

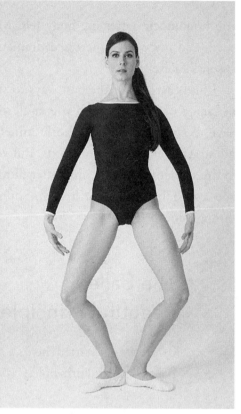

2
Think Like a Swan

The key to elegant posture is keeping your neck long and your shoulders down. Sometimes, in an effort to keep your chest open or shoulders back, you might tense and pull up your shoulders. Instead, think about opening your chest, keeping your neck long and graceful like a swan, and gently pulling your shoulder blades down into your back. You are lifting through your chest and center as you push your shoulders down.

3
Work Within Your Range of Motion

The easiest way to hurt your joints is by forcing your range of motion. Be mindful of the range of motion in your knees and hips and be certain that when you take a standing plié (a bend in the knees; see "Your Ballet Primer" on page 49), your knees line up right over your toes. My joints are very flexible, and your position may not be as open as mine. That's okay! Be mindful of what works best for your body to protect your joints, and take it slow.

4

Change the Shape of Your Legs
by Stretching Your Knees

When I talk about the concept of stretching long through your muscles during an exercise, this is what I mean. Learning to work with your knees fully straight and in a lifted, strong position will radically change the shape of your legs and take years off of your figure. Work with your knees either straight or bent—no in between. When doing any straight-leg exercises on the mat, like my Inner Thigh Series, it's important to keep your knee pulled up (but not locked) and engaged while stretching long through the leg. The same is true for my standing exercises—pay close attention to the bend and stretch in your knees. Not only will this help you shape your legs beautifully and get rid of saggy over-the-knee skin, but it will strengthen your joints and protect them.

* * *

One final note before we get started: make sure to read through the workouts first so you can familiarize yourself with the movements and pace. You can even "mark" the steps before you begin, testing the shape of your body in each movement without fully exerting and performing the full exercise. Dancers do this all the time when learning new combinations—marking the steps first. Marking is like writing a rough draft or taking notes with your body and your muscle memory, and it's a great way to get familiar with new steps and movements. Discovering a new way of moving and working the body may seem awkward at first, but trust me, you'll get the hang of it in no time.

Chapter 5

The Classic 60-Minute Ballet Beautiful Workout

This chapter highlights the Classic Ballet Beautiful Workout, a comprehensive, hour-long workout that targets the upper body, center, arms, legs, and butt. The Classic is the best place to learn how the different elements of Ballet Beautiful are put into practice. This all-over body workout, with a focus on toning exercises through mat and resistance work, is a totally doable workout—for the beginner, intermediate, or trained expert! Anyone can benefit from how it targets and strengthens your ballet muscles, transforming the shape of your lines. I used a version of this workout daily when I was dancing with the New York City Ballet to keep me centered and strong.

Here's an outline of how it works. After a gentle five-minute stretch, you begin to target the five critical areas of a ballerina body:

1. *Back of the legs and butt:* I love the way my Bridge Series gets the muscles in your legs and butt working—it's an absolute killer! The Reverse Bridge is also an awesome workout for the butt and legs. It's great for strengthening your center too!

2. *Abdominals:* Get ready to tone and strengthen deep through your stomach and center.

3. *Inner thighs:* This workout targets that hard-to-reach area along the inside of the leg that is critical for shaping a ballerina's legs.

4. *Outer thighs:* These exercises target and tone the muscles on the hard-to-reach part of the outside of your hip, thigh, and butt, lengthening the lines of your legs and getting rid of cellulite.

5. *Standing work with arms:* These fun, graceful standing exercises include low-impact, cardiovascular elements to sculpt lean, toned, feminine arms and to tighten and lengthen the entire body. They are also a fun way to practice your plié and port de bras while you work out!

I adore the way that these Classic exercises continue to strengthen and tone my physique and let me stay connected to my love of dance—even on days when I can't get to a ballet studio! Because we are not using weights or equipment, the muscles we are building are long and lean—these exercises will never make you bulky. They may require a few more reps than you're used to, but I can promise you that it will be worth it!

For each movement in the different targeted areas, you will do four sets of eight counts, a classic ballet workout. You'll start on the right side, complete a sequence, then switch to the left. You will also be stretching between the movements; don't skip this stretch! Stretching as you go is so important. It will help you get the most out of every exercise. Remember too that you can use the stretches to modify the exercises. If you are a beginner and just getting started, you may want to take more time to stretch during the exercises and perform fewer reps. If you are advanced and want a more challenging workout, you can leave the stretching to the end of each section.

Throughout the exercises, I've offered adjustments (✽). These are modifications you can use to make a movement either more challenging or less challenging, depending on whether you are a beginner or looking for a more difficult workout. Watch for adjustments for beginners indicated by **/B.**, and for advanced indicated by **/A.** My Ballet Beautiful principles are marked by the Ballet Beautiful logo.

At the end of the mat work, we will transition into the Standing Series, which is a quick cardio blast and a terrific upper body workout.

All this adds up to a complete-body workout that tones, strengthens, lengthens, and satisfies! By targeting, isolating, and exhausting your ballet muscles, you will see immediate results. Get ready for the transformation and your incredible new Ballet Beautiful body!

Katherine on Transforming Her Body

I noticed a change almost immediately when I started Ballet Beautiful. My body felt different. My butt and muscles became more toned. And I discovered muscles that I never knew I had—after just two weeks! The look and feel was totally different and I felt so proud of my results.

REMEMBER THE BB PRINCIPLES

1. Stomach pulled in toward your spine, center engaged

2. Neck long and graceful—like a swan!

3. Work within your range of motion to protect your joints

4. Build long, lean muscle by stretching the knees

You will be sipping lots of water throughout each workout—whether the Classic or the Cardio Blasts—to make sure your body stays hydrated, so keep your water bottle nearby.

A Note on Adjustments

Remember: this workout is not for professional dancers. It's for anyone looking to sculpt a body shape that is powerful yet feminine from the comfort and privacy of their own home. You can benefit from the Ballet Beautiful workout regardless of your experience, your current workout routine, or the number of years you have or have not been dancing. In most cases, I offer ways to modify the workout to make it simpler or more challenging. Look for the ✳ as you go!

Simple Stretch (5 Minutes)

Every Ballet Beautiful workout begins with a simple stretch to open and release the muscles in your back, hips, and legs. Hold stretches for anywhere from 10 to 90 seconds, depending on how much time you have available and how tight your body feels. (See pages 55–61 for refreshers on these stretches.)

Classic Hamstring Stretch

a Sit on the floor or your mat, legs in front of you. Bend your left knee toward your hips and extend your right leg out long on the floor in front of you.

b Extend your body forward toward your right foot, keeping your knee straight. Reach toward your right foot with both hands as the muscles begin to open

through the back of your hamstring and leg.

c Don't worry about whether your left hip reaches the floor or about how low it is; everyone's hips are different. Your hips will loosen and open over time.

d Repeat on the other side.

Hip Opener

a Begin seated on the mat with your legs in front of you.

b Bend your right knee by bringing your right foot in toward your hip. Extend your left leg long behind you on the mat. You can use your arms to lift and brace your body.

c Sit up high and open through the chest, pulling your stomach in.

d Gently bend toward the bent knee for a stretch through the spine. Your hips may lift off the floor, and that's okay; your range of movement and your flexibility will change the more you stretch.

e Repeat on the other side.

Ballet Beautiful *Bridge Series*

Back of the Legs and Butt (15-20 Minutes)

My longtime clients love the Ballet Beautiful Bridge Series because they know how well these exercises work! The set below is a terrific combination of my favorite Bridge exercises to sculpt and tighten the legs, butt, hips, center, and thighs.

STARTING POSITION: I always begin my Classic Ballet Beautiful workout on the mat, just as I would begin any warm-up for a show.

Lie on your back and bend your knees so that they form a right angle with your pelvis. Press your shoulders and upper back into the floor and pull your stomach in tight. Your arms can stay down by your sides on the mat, or you can tuck your hands under your head. This exercise is all about the butt, center, and legs,

so find a position that is comfortable and relaxed for your upper body and arms. Keep your feet together, on the floor, with your knees closed together to engage the inner thigh. Lift your hips high, pushing your pelvic bone up toward the ceiling while keeping your stomach tight. Be careful not to arch your back—pushing high with your hips and pelvis will help to avoid this. You will be doing 4 sets of 8 counts, at a moderate pace, for 15 to 20 minutes.

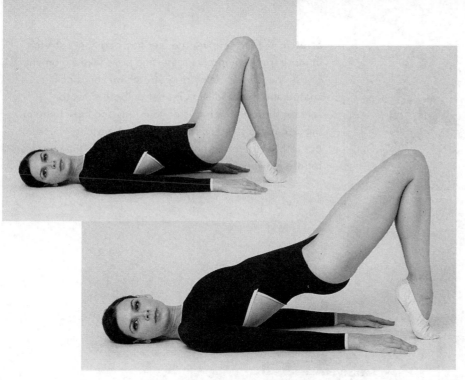
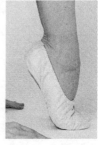

Classic Ballet Beautiful Bridge

a From the starting position, place your feet flat on the floor (or bring your toes up onto demi-pointe for a more advanced version).

b Lift up your hips and butt.

c Lower your back without quite letting your hips and butt touch the mat. *8 counts, 4 sets.*

d Make sure you keep your stomach engaged to take the stress out of your lower back and spine, squeeze your butt as you lift, and keep your knees closed to engage your inner thighs and turnout muscles. Also, keep your upper body relaxed—and don't forget to breathe!

e Hold the position high on the final count of the final set (the eighth count of the fourth set).

f From this high, lifted position, squeeze the muscles in your butt and inner thighs, pull your stomach in, and lift higher in a pulse. Try to keep your knees together to connect to your inner thighs (it's a challenge). You will feel the muscles in your back and the insides of your legs and butt engaging and beginning to burn. *8 counts, 4 sets.*

✴ *For a greater challenge*, do this movement from demi-pointe (as in the photo), with your foot on the floor arched, remembering to keep your ankles very steady and the work in your upper legs and butt. This will help you achieve a larger range of motion, which is more challenging. You can move directly into the next exercise without stopping to stretch.

Stretch: ✱ **/B.** Keeping the feet flat, beginners stretch at more frequent intervals, starting now. Take a moment to use the Classic Hamstring Stretch on your back or seated and a seated Hip Opener on both sides to release through the backs of your legs and hips. Keep in mind that this stretch is not meant to be a long pause but rather a quick and gentle way to release the muscles before moving on to the next movements.

Butterfly

a Return to the starting bridge position and lift your hips high, with your knees together and your feet flat or on demi-pointe.

b Keeping your hips very lifted and still, open and close your knees in a butterfly movement, emphasizing the squeeze as you bring your knees together. Keeping your center firm will help support your back. *8 counts, 4 sets.*

✱ **/B.** If you are a beginner, take a stretch here. **/A.** If you are more advanced, you can move directly into the next set. This is true for most of the exercises. Essentially, if you want more of a challenge, keep going without pausing. If you need a break and feel stiff or tired, do a quick five-minute stretch.

✱ **/A.** Do this exercise from demi-pointe.

Remember to pull in your stomach and connect to your center, relax through your shoulders, keep your arms flat on the mat, and breathe!

Now begin another set of the Classic Bridge:

a Return to the starting position.

b Bring your knees together and lift high through the hips.

c Lower and lift, with your stomach pulled in tight. *8 counts, 4 sets.*

Stretch: Repeat the Classic Hamstring Stretch and the Hip Opener on both legs, or try the advanced stretch for the hamstrings and hips.

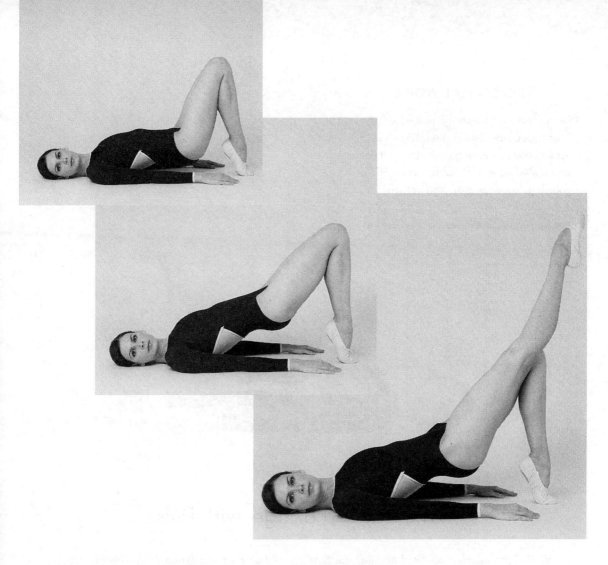

One-Legged Bridge

a Lift into the Classic Bridge, with your knees together and your hips high, feet flat or on demi-pointe.

b Extend one leg off the mat and straight up at a 90-degree angle, then drop the leg to a 45-degree angle so that your knees are level. ✳ Keep the extended leg at a 90-degree angle from the hip.)

c Pull your stomach in and lower your hips so that they are not quite touching the mat. Keep your leg steady and extended as you raise and lower your hips. If you begin to feel this in your back, tighten your center to stabilize your back. *8 counts, 4 sets.* Hold up on the last count of the last set.

TIPS ON MAT WORK

Do not actually touch the mat when you lower your hips during the bridge. Go up and down, keeping your stomach flat and pulled in, your shoulders relaxed, your legs squeezing in. And breathe!

One-Legged Bridge, with Pulse

a Pull your stomach in tight and lift your hips from the highest position; your right leg should still be extended off the mat and straight up at a 90-degree angle. (✻ *IA.* Drop your leg down to 45 degrees).

b Now squeeze through your butt, pulling your stomach in tight as you lift and pulse higher in the same position. This works your inner thigh and butt.

c Keep breathing! You will feel the standing leg working hard! *8 counts, 4 sets.*

✻ *For more challenge,* (1) do this exercise on demi-pointe (flat foot for more moderate challenge) or (2) extend your leg at a 45-degree angle (90-degree angle for more moderate challenge).

Stretch: Do the Classic Hamstring Stretch and Hip Opener; change legs and repeat on the other side. To mix it up a bit at this point, do the Classic Hamstring Stretch on your back and the Hip Opener while seated.

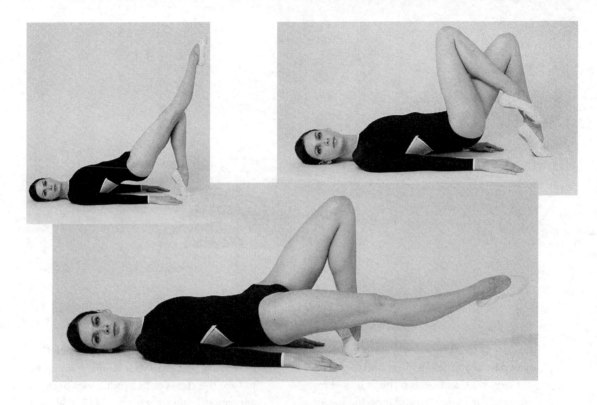

Bridge with Can-Can Kick!

✳ **/A.** This is an optional advanced bridge for those of you who want a further challenge!

a Begin in the Classic, One-Legged Bridge position: feet together, knees together, stomach in, hips lifted high (see photo, page 79).

b Extend your right leg into the air and drop your hips down, bending your right knee.

c Extend your right leg up again to the ceiling at 90 degrees, just like a can-can kick. (✳ **/A.** Lower the working leg toward the standing knee at a 45-degree angle, with knees together. This angle is slightly more challenging for the butt and standing leg.)

d Lower your hips again, bending your right knee in. Lift and repeat.

e Hold up on the final count of 8 for 10 seconds. Release down. *8 counts, 4 sets.* Change legs and repeat on the other side.

✳ **Optional hold:** To make this exercise more challenging, lower the working leg toward the mat, keeping your hips high and engaging through your center. Hold this extended position for 2 sets of 8 to really take it to the next level!

✳ **/B.** Beginners can start with 2 sets of 8.

Stretch: Classic Hamstring and Seated Hip Opener.

Extended Bridge

This part of the Bridge Series targets the lower part of your hamstrings and the backs of your legs, butt, and center. This is one of my favorite ways to tighten and tone the backs of the legs to get ready for shorts and bikinis!

STARTING POSITION: This is similar to the Classic Bridge, but with the legs extended out on the mat and away from your butt and hips.

a Begin by lying on your back with your knees and feet together, as with the Classic Bridge.

b Now walk your feet away from your hips so that your feet are extended beyond your knees at a 45-degree angle.

c Pull your stomach in and lift your hips off the floor, pushing your pelvic bone high toward the ceiling to prevent any arch in your spine. You can place your feet flat on the floor or bring your toes up onto demi-pointe for a more advanced version. *8 counts, 4 sets.* Hold on the final count of 8.

d There are several things to keep in mind: Make sure you keep your stomach engaged to take the stress out of your lower back and spine. Squeeze your butt as you lift and keep your knees closed to engage your inner thighs and turnout muscles. As you lift and lower your hips, make sure they don't touch the mat. And keep your upper body relaxed—don't forget to breathe!

e Hold up high on the final count of the final set (the eighth count of the fourth set). The higher you raise your hips, the more range of motion you will create. Squeeze through your inner thigh and butt, pulling your stomach in.

f Now lift your hips and butt higher, in a pulse. *8 counts, 4 sets.* Hold up on the last count of 8.

✳ **/B.** Beginners can stretch here!

Butterfly Extended Bridge

Return to the starting Extended Bridge position and lift your hips high, with your knees together and feet flat or on demi-pointe. Keep your hips lifted high as you open and close your knees. Emphasize the closed position here to really engage your inner thighs. Keep your hips steady and your stomach engaged. *8 counts, 4 sets.*

Stretch: Classic Hamstring (seated) and Hip Opener, both sides.

Extended Bridge on One Leg

a From the starting position in the
Extended Bridge, lift your hips into the air
with your feet and knees together and
your legs extended out on the mat
(✳ **/ B.** feet flat for beginners,
/ A. demi-pointe for advanced).

b Now lift one leg into the air (✳ at 90
degrees for beginners; at 45 degrees,
with knees together, for advanced).

c With your leg extended into the air, lower
your hips down, not quite touching the
mat. Now lift your hips again as you raise
your butt back into the air. Engage
through your stomach and stay relaxed
through your upper body. Lower and lift
your hips without arching your back.
8 counts, 4 sets. Repeat on other side.

Stretch: Classic Hamstring Stretch (seated),
Hip Opener (seated), and Upper Body
Stretch with Port de Bras (seated).

Reverse Bridge Series:
Legs, Center, and Butt (10 Minutes)

In this section, you will continue to work on your legs, center, and butt, but on your stomach rather than your back. If you are working on a hard surface, you may need extra padding under your pelvic bone for these—try a towel or roll up part of your mat.

STARTING POSITION: After releasing the muscles in your arms and legs with the seated stretches following the Extended Bridge on One Leg, you are ready to get into position for the Reverse Bridge.

a Go down onto your stomach on your mat, with your arms to the sides and your legs stretched out long.

b Pull your stomach in to engage your center and open through the chest as you

bring your arms in front of your body to first position on the mat.

c Bend your knees and bring your heels together.

d Keeping your neck long and your gaze downward, lift slightly through your back and use the muscles in your legs, stomach, and butt to lift both knees off the ground and into the Reverse Bridge.

Reverse Bridge

a Your knees will be slightly open in attitude as you lift the tops of your thighs off the floor. Keep your stomach pulled in and stay engaged through your center.

b Lower your legs back to the floor, keeping your toes together and your legs in the same attitude position. Keep your upper body relaxed.

c Pull in through your center again and lift your legs off the floor. You should really feel this through your butt and inner thigh! *8 counts, 2 sets.*

✳ /A. For an advanced version, do 4 sets of 8 counts, then go directly to the next exercise.

Stretch: Classic Hamstring Stretch.

Reverse Bridge Lift

a From the starting position for the Reverse Bridge, return to the Reverse Bridge, with your legs in the air.

b Pull in through your stomach and squeeze through the backs of your legs and butt.

c From this position, lift your legs slightly higher, then lower them back down slightly to the starting position with your legs in the air. This slight lifted pulse engages the muscles in the back, insides of the legs, and butt. *8 counts, 2 sets.*

✳ /A. For advanced, do 4 sets of 8 counts, remembering to keep your stomach pulled in and working.

Stretch: Classic Hamstring Stretch and Upper Body Stretch with Port de Bras.

Reverse Bridge on One Leg

a With your legs stretched out long on the mat, bend your right knee into attitude and bend your arms into a folded first position on the mat.

b Pull in with your stomach and lift your right knee off the floor, extending your leg higher into the air. Keep your left knee straight on the ground and pull in to engage your center.

c Lift your back leg in attitude higher into the air and pull in through your stomach.

d Lower the working leg slightly, then lift again, engaging through your butt and inner thigh. *8 counts, 4 sets.*

Reverse Bridge with One-Leg Lift

a From the starting position for Reverse Bridge on One Leg, extend one leg back into attitude, with your knee slightly open.

b Pull your arms into a folded first position on the mat in front of you; pull in and engage through your stomach.

c Lift your back leg into the air in attitude, then lift slightly higher into a pulse. *8 counts, 4 sets.*

If you need a break here, take a stretch for the upper body and hamstrings and have some water. (✳ If your muscles are feeling great, you can move directly into the arabesque extensions.)

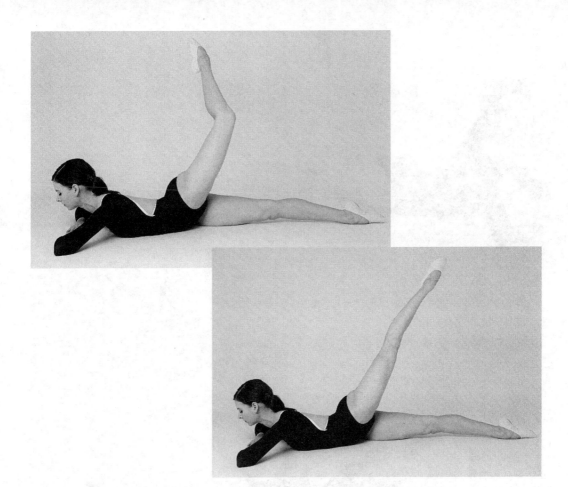

Reverse Bridge with Arabesque Extension

a The starting position is the same as for Reverse Bridge on One Leg and Reverse Bridge with One-Leg Lifts. Begin from the One-Leg Reverse Bridge. Lift your right leg back into attitude, lifting your knee off the floor and pulling in through your stomach. Extend the working knee and stretch your back leg into arabesque.

b Bend the working knee back into attitude and then stretch and extend the knee again, stretching back into arabesque.

c Remember to keep your upper body relaxed, your neck long, and your stomach engaged. Fully stretch your knee in arabesque each time. *8 counts, 2 sets.*

* **IA.** For the advanced version, do 4 sets of 8 counts, remembering to keep your stomach pulled in and working.

Reverse Bridge with Arabesque Lift

a Return to a Reverse Bridge with Arabesque Extension, with your stomach engaged and the working leg lifted into the air and stretched into an arabesque.

b Now lower the leg slightly before lifting it higher into arabesque, then back onto the mat. *8 counts, 4 sets.*

Stretch: Classic Hamstring Stretch and Upper Body Stretch with Port de Bras.

Repeat the last five exercises on the other leg.

Abdominals (10 Minutes)

In this section, we are transitioning into work on the abdominals, with a focus on the lower abdomen. Your lowers abs are the part of your stomach muscles that run deep through your center. They are a hard part of the stomach to tighten and tone, and that's why I like to focus on them! Think about the area just between your hipbones and pull it in tight. This is your lower abdomen.

Here is the classic starting position for getting connected to your lower abs.

STARTING POSTION: From a seated position on the floor, extend your legs out long. Pull your stomach in toward your spine and extend your upper body behind you, engaging with your center and taking a slight bend in your knees. Lift your arms out in front of you into first position. Make sure you have plenty of extra padding under your tailbone—

I sometimes roll up my mat or towel for more comfort. Remember the principle of keeping the stomach pulled in tight and engaged—it's important that you pull in and scoop through the stomach as you perform these abs exercises to get a flat, defined center and not one overly built up with muscles.

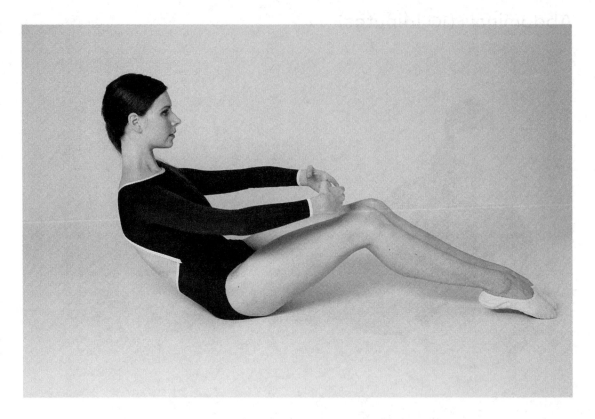

Classic Ballet Beautiful Abs

The range of motion on this exercise is small, but the movement deeply engages the abs. As you gain strength from the workout, your range of motion may increase.

a Get started by extending back to a position where your abs are engaged and pulling your stomach in tight. Pull your upper body back by about 30 degrees and pull in to engage your lower abs.

b Lean back slightly, pulling in through your abs as you lower and lift your upper body, making certain not to lift your torso up to a position that allows your stomach to relax.

Keep your head and arms lifted and stay relaxed throughout your upper body so that you don't strain your neck. *8 counts, 3 sets.* Hold on the last count of 8.

✳ If you are just getting started and have pain in your lower back, start with one set of 10, take a break, and then try 10 more. When the abdominal muscles get fatigued and give out, your lower back sometimes takes over; at this point, stop, stretch, and start again. Working with fewer reps allows you to increase your strength over time and build up to the full number of reps.

Classic Pulse

As with Classic Ballet Beautiful Abs, the range of motion here is small—in fact, it's even smaller!—but this exercise is very effective.

a Hold back into the extended position, arms rounded in first position in front, and pull your stomach in tight.

b Stay extended through your spine, with your chin slightly down as you open your arms to second position and pulse back toward the floor, pulling in through your lower abs. Don't curve your shoulders or hunch, but feel yourself lifted as your core is engaged. *8 counts, 3 sets.*

✳ **/B.** If you are just getting started, put your arms behind your knees or keep them resting behind you so that you can focus on your abs and on pulling them in. If you feel weak through your center or are experiencing lower back pain, go slowly on these. You can begin with sets of 5 or 10 reps and stretch as you go. As you build up strength through your center, add more reps—always remembering to listen to your body's needs.

✳ **/A.** For an advanced version extend the arms side in second position.

Seated Ab Stretch

a Begin seated on the mat. Pull your legs into a comfortable crossed position.

b Place your hands on your knees and pull in through your stomach as you arch your back.

c Sit up and take a port de bras with both arms up to fifth position (hands together with the arms curved above your head).

d Repeat the port de bras stretch, dropping one arm to a low fourth position, curved by your stomach, and lifting the other arm up and over your head to fourth position, extending up and over to the side.

e Repeat on the other side.

Ballet Twist from Side to Side

I love the way this exercise lets me quickly connect to my center. This is one of my favorites to do before ballet class or a rehearsal to quickly heat up and engage my abs. These movements work the obliques, the sides, and the center part of your abdominals.

a Start from the Classic Ballet Beautiful Abs position, with your knees slightly bent, your arms in first position, and your stomach pulled in tight. Extend your legs straight out in front of you on the mat.

* / **B.** Beginners may keep their knees bent as in the Classic Ballet Beautiful Abs position.

b Extend back about 30 degrees, twist your upper body, and pull your stomach in tight,

scooping your lowers abs in toward your center.

c Keep pulling your abs in as you change sides, rotating from the right to the left. You can find a nice rhythm here. I find that moving a bit more slowly and taking a beat on each side to truly pull in and connect to my abs makes this exercise more challenging and rewarding!

d Keep your arms in first position and really scoop with your core. Think about pulling that stomach in as you lower and twist. This is a difficult exercise, and when you're exerting, the urge is to push the stomach out rather than pull it in. *10 counts, 4 sets.*

One-Leg Extension for the Lower Abs

a Stretch your legs out long on the mat.

b Pull back and pull your stomach in tight, with your arms in first position.

c Lift one leg off the floor about 10 to 20 degrees.

d Keeping the leg lifted, lean back, pulling your stomach in and lifting to the starting position. Note that you are working your abs here—the movement is in your core, not in your leg. Your leg should stay steady, lifted at 10 to 20 degrees.
8 counts, 4 sets. Repeat on the other side.

✳ If your lower back or hip flexors are sensitive, you can keep this leg extended out but on the floor, as in the starting position. It's still a great ab workout!

Stretch: Sit up, release your rib cage with a Seated Ab Stretch, and relax your upper body.

One-Leg Extension with a Twist

This exercise combines the movements from Ballet Twists and the One-Leg Extensions.

a Repeat the One-Leg Extension, but this time, when you lower your leg, twist to one side (the same side as your raised leg), pulling in tight through your abs and side, and then return to the center.

b Be certain to keep your stomach pulled in and engaged and to stay relaxed through the upper body. *8 counts, 2 sets.* Change sides.

✳ You can modify this exercise by keeping the working leg on the floor.

Stretch: Sit up, release your rib cage with a Seated Ab Stretch, and relax your upper body.

One-Leg Extension with a Twist and Hold

a In the same position as for One-Leg Extension with a Twist, lift one arm high to fourth position and twist toward the opposite, raised leg.

b Lower down your torso, pulling your stomach in tight. Remember, you are working your center here. Your leg should remain raised and quiet, as should your arms. *8 counts, 2 sets.*

c Repeat on the other side.

Inner Thighs (12 Minutes)

Ballet dancers are constantly engaging their inner thighs because so much of the dancing is done from a turned-out position. From your plié tendus at the barre to the perfect balance in fifth position on pointe, the inner thighs are lifting and working nonstop. This series of movements tightens and tones the inner thighs to build the long, lean muscles that define a ballet leg.

Classic Inner Thigh Lift

STARTING POSITION: Lie on your mat on your right side, with your right leg extended down along the mat. Your left leg will be on top. Bend your knee and place your left foot either in front of your bottom leg or behind it, with your foot lifted on demi-pointe or flat. The working leg here is the bottom leg—that is where the focus is. Your upper body should be relaxed; lean on your right elbow or keep your upper body down on the mat, stretching your right arm out long. Pull your stomach in to engage your center and stretch through your bottom knee.

a Keeping your bottom knee straight and lifted, raise and lower your bottom leg up and down. *8 counts, 4 sets.* Hold your leg up on the last count of 8.

Classic Inner Thigh Lift with High Extension

a From the highest point in the Classic Inner Thigh Lift, lift even higher, with a quick pulse up and down. *8 counts, 4 sets.* Hold your leg up on the last count of 8.

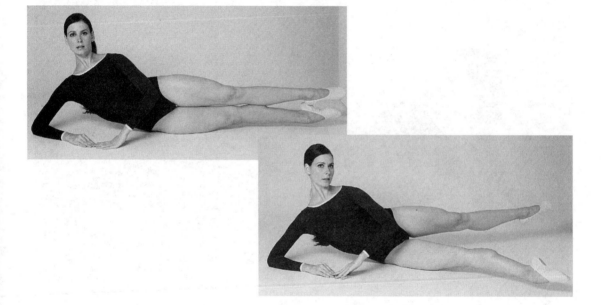

Inner Thigh Extensions from First to Fourth

a Keeping both knees straight extend the top leg out, taking the legs to first position. Engage through the stomach and stay relaxed through the chest.

b Stretch both knees and engage through the inner thighs as you extend the bottom leg to the front and the top leg back into fourth position.

c Bring the legs back to first position and extend to fourth again, lifting through the knees while engaging your center. *8 counts, 4 sets.*

✳ */A.* Hold this extended fourth position for another 4 sets of 8.

Classic Inner Thigh Lift—Repeated

Bring the legs back to the starting position and repeat another set of the Classic Inner Thigh Lifts. Again, you will feel this in your upper thighs and butt. Stay centered and engaged in your abs. *8 counts, 4 sets.*

Inner Thigh Stretch

a Sit up and extend one leg out to the side, as if preparing for a center split, and reach toward your foot.

b Bend your other leg into a passé position, slightly to the front.

c Stretch the knee of the extended leg and lift the opposite arm up into a port de bras, curved above your head, reaching up and over toward the extended leg and stretching through your upper body. Curve your other arm low in front of you. Release through the side and back.

d Switch legs and repeat on the other side.

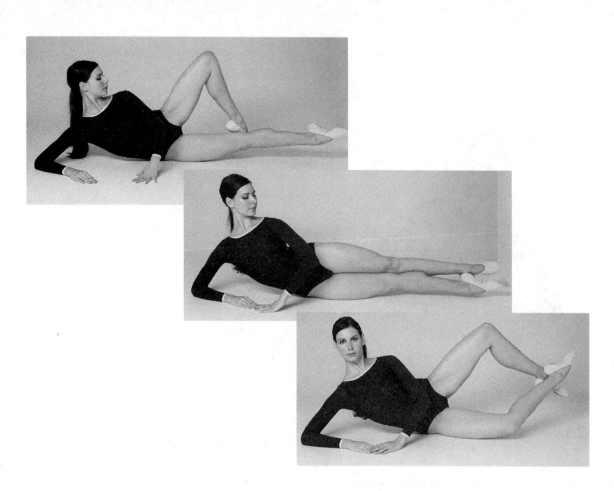

Attitude Extension

a Get down on your side in the starting position, as in the Classic Inner Thigh Lift.

b Bend both knees into attitude and lift them off the floor, with your right foot in front. Engage your stomach and keep your chest open.

c Straighten both knees and extend your legs into fifth position in the air on your side.

d Bend your knees again and return to attitude; then extend again. Keep your chest open and your stomach engaged. *8 counts, 2 sets.*

* **/B.** Since this exercise is more advanced, beginners can start with one set of 8 reps, or they can even try bending and stretching the bottom leg only, leaving the top leg as a balance (as in the top photo on this page).

Stretch: Do an Inner Thigh Stretch, then repeat on the other side.

Outer Thighs (10–15 Minutes)

This series of movements is a focused workout for the outside of the legs, the butt, and the outside of the thighs. These are terrific mat exercises that tighten and tone the muscles while elongating the limbs.

STARTING POSITION: On your right side, stretch your legs out long on the mat. Find a comfortable position for your upper body. Bend your top arm in toward your center, and stretch the arm on the floor out long. Extend both knees straight. You will complete the entire sequence on your right side, then switch to your left.

Outer Thigh Battement Tendu Lift in Parallel

a Point your foot as you lift, then lower your top leg in the air while keeping your hips in parallel.

b Stay stretched long through your lifted leg, engage with your core, and keep your hips turned in. And don't forget to keep breathing—this is difficult. You will start to feel a burning sensation in your outer hip and butt. *8 counts, 4 sets.* Hold your leg up on the last count of 8.

✳ **/B.** Beginners can take a Seated Hip Stretch here.

Tendu Lift in Parallel with High Extension

a Lift the working leg even higher from the highest point in the previous exercise, keeping your knee straight and your stomach pulled in tight.

b Keeping your hips parallel and your toe pointed and facing down toward the floor, lift higher and lower slightly. *8 counts, 4 sets.* Hold your leg up on the last count of 8.

Outer Thigh Rond de Jambe en l'Air

a From the lifted position in the previous exercise, circle the working leg in front in a Rond de Jambe en l'Air. This isn't a large movement. Visualize yourself drawing a small circle in the air with your working toe and leg. Your working leg lifts up, around to the back, forward, and up again.

b Keep your leg in the air the entire time and your hips parallel—think about dropping your toe toward the floor.

c Reverse the direction of the circular motion. *8 counts, 4 sets.*

Remember, if your muscles are not burning, they're not working. You can always stop and take a five-minute stretch, but otherwise—keep going!

Battement Tendu Lift in Parallel—Repeated

Repeat Outer Thigh Battement Tendu Lifts in Parallel, lifting and lowering even higher. Make sure this is a controlled movement—you don't need to "throw" or force your leg into the air. Your legs will really start to burn now. *8 counts, 4 sets.*

Stretch: Seated Hip Opener or Classic Hamstring Stretch. These stretches from the beginning of the Classic Workout will feel great after the hard work you're putting your thighs and butt through here!

Take a quick, three-minute break and stretch. Open your hips, move around, and relax. Take a sip of water, then come back down for one last set on the same side.

Fondu Side in Parallel

a Return to the basic Battement Tendu Lift on the right side, legs stretched out.

b Lift your top leg and extend it out high into a tendu in parallel side, then bend it into an attitude parallel as you bring it in.

c Stretch and extend back out into a fondue. This fondue movement is similar to what you did with your leg in the can-can kick in the Bridge Series. *8 counts, 4 sets.*

Note: Throughout this exercise, remember to engage through your stomach, keep breathing, relax, and stay stable in your upper body resting on the mat. Keep your top toe

continues

Fondu Side in Parallel *(continued)*

pointing down toward the mat to help guide your hips into a truly parallel position. Your muscle is fatigued now, so expect to be really feeling it.

Stretch: Take a break to take a sip of water, move a little, and stretch your inner thighs and hamstrings.

Repeat all of the movements in the Outer Thighs Series on the other leg, remembering to stay connected to your center by pulling your abs in tight. (✳ *IA.* Lift your leg higher and keep your hip parallel to make the lifts more challenging.)

Standing Series with Arms (5–10 Minutes)

The Standing Series is a quick (only 5 to 10 minutes!), fun, and graceful workout that gets your heart pumping and helps get the muscles you've just been working to release in an active way. It's also a terrific upper body workout that builds and tones muscles without making them bulky. Because we are standing, we are going to use our basic ballet vocabulary (see "Your Ballet Primer" on page 49).

If you've ever been to a ballet, I'm sure you've noticed the incredibly graceful way dancers carry their arms. They're both strong and weightless, with impeccable posture. The movements in this series will give you a terrific way to sculpt your arms and connect more deeply to your center. Take care not to arch your back (you will be engaging your center, remember?), and keep a beautiful lift through your elbows, without lifting your shoulders. (The arm positions are described on page 51.)

Tendu Arabesque in Plié

STARTING POSITION: Your legs are nice and warm from the mat work, so you can get right into the Tendu Arabesque. This is a terrific exercise for toning your legs while building strength through your center and creating better posture. The Tendu Arabesque is in many ways like a graceful ballet version of a lunge—but one that will not bulk your thighs!

a Begin by standing on your right leg in a ballet lunge, with your right knee slightly bent into a demi-plié and your left leg stretched out behind you in an arabesque.

b With your stomach pulled in and your arms lowered down to your sides, you can keep your back foot on the floor. Your weight is over the ball of your front foot. Keep your neck long and your stomach engaged. If you feel unsteady, improvise your own ballet barre by holding on to a chair or a wall.

c Bend your standing knee slightly deeper in demi-plié, with a slight pulsing motion. *8 counts, 4 sets.*

Arabesque Lift with Swan Arms

a From the starting position, stretch your standing knee straight and lift your back leg off the floor into arabesque en l'air. Don't worry about how high your back leg is here—you can start with your foot just off the floor and lift higher in time as you gain strength and stability.

b As you lift your back leg high, pull in through your stomach, engaging your stomach and center.

c Lift your arms up high above your head into a V position and stretch both knees.

d Lower your back knee down to the floor, returning to your starting position, a ballet lunge. Bring your arms down at the same time without collapsing your back and upper body. This movement works your legs, core, and arms, but the main focus is on your arms. Make sure the raising and lowering of them is focused and concentrated. *8 counts, 4 sets.*

Stretch: / **B.** Beginners may stretch here (Standing Stretch for Legs), while the more advanced */* **A.** continue directly to the next movement.

Arabesque Plié en l'Air

a Bring your back leg down into a tendu arabesque and bend your standing knee.

b Lower your arms to first position (rounded in front of you, elbows lifted), keeping your stomach engaged, your neck long, and your chest open. And do not arch your back!

c With your arms staying in first position in front of you and your standing knee positioned over your toes, lift your back leg into an arabesque en l'air, keeping your standing knee bent.

d Pulse here in a demi-plié while keeping your back leg lifted in arabesque. *8 counts, 4 sets.*

✳ Use a chair or wall for extra support if you feel unsteady.

Stretch: **I B.** Beginners can take a Standing Stretch here.

Low Arabesque Lunge

This exercise really works the butt and thigh!

a From the Tendu Arabesque Lift, drop your back leg onto the floor, as shown, keeping your arms in first position, your right leg back, your chest very open, and your front knee in demi-plié.

b Slide your back leg out onto the floor in arabesque as you deepen your plié into a low lunge.

❋ **/ B.** If you're a beginner, you can keep your arms in first position as you extend down, as shown.

/ A. For an advanced version of the movement, take a twist through the spine as you take your arms into third position.

c Take care that your standing knee is over your toe. Deepen the standing knee slightly in plié and pulse there. Extend through your spine and keep your neck relaxed. *8 counts, 2 sets.*

Stretch: Slowly lift your upper body as you stretch the standing knee into a tendu arabesque with straight knees.

continues

Repeat Tendu Arabesque in Plié, Arabesque Lift with Swan Arms, and Arabesque Plié en l'Air on the other side. *8 counts, 4 sets.*

Plié Tendu Front

STARTING POSITION: Start by extending your right leg into a tendu front, lifting up through both knees. Make sure your front toe is pointed and that both knees are fully straight. Pull your stomach in tight and open your arms to third position by bending your left arm into first position, curved in front of you, and extending your right arm into second position.

a Bend your standing knee into a plié and slide your front leg out along the floor.

b Pull in through your stomach and reach your left arm down toward your right foot. On your standing leg, keep your knee over your toes.

c Pulse here in plié, with a slight deepening through the standing knee. Keep your arms steady and your stomach engaged. Working in this lowered position really challenges the muscles in your legs, butt, and center. *8 counts, 4 sets.*

Plié Dégagé Lift Front

These are very challenging movements, so we will only do one set of 8. Be careful to use your center and engage your ab muscles. Also, do not arch your back and fully bend and stretch your knees.

STARTING POSITION: From the beginning position for Plié Tendu Front, pull in through your stomach to engage your center and lift your arms up high to third position as you lift your upper body and stretch and lift both knees. This is a great ab workout too!

a As you stretch up with your legs and upper body, you will pass through a Tendu Front. Then, as your leg lifts off the floor and extends into the air, you will move from a tendu into a Dégagé en l'Air.

b Keep your stomach engaged and do not arch your back.

c From this lifted dégagé position, carefully lower the working leg onto the floor, again in Tendu Front, and bend the standing knee back down into a plié.

continues

Plié Dégagé Lift Front (continued)

d Now lift and stretch again through Tendu Front into the air, with your front foot off the ground.

e Keep your neck long and remember your posture—do not let your upper body collapse as you lift and lower.
8 counts, 1 set.

Stretch: Standing Stretch.

Repeat the entire Tendu Front Series on the other side.

Final Stretch and Reverence

Congrats on finishing such a challenging workout! We will close with a final stretch to release your muscles and cool down and also with a reverence.

Stretch: Classic Hamstring Stretch and Hip Opener. Let's finish this stretch-out with a center split (remember, it doesn't have to be 180 degrees). Hold this position for just a few seconds (or a few minutes if you have more time), and then stand for the reverence.

Reverence

Begin the reverence with a port de bras of the arms to fifth position. Lift your arms up over your head, keeping your center engaged and your posture very erect. Now take your right leg to Tendu Front, with your arms in third position.

Lift through your upper body and engage your stomach. Bend your supporting leg as you take your left arm into port de bras low. Lift back to tendu with a straight knee and change sides. Repeat on the other side. Now take a tendu in arabesque with the arms in third position.

continues

WHAT IS A REVERENCE?

A reverence in ballet is like a curtsy or a bow. It is a way of saying thank-you through movement and of showing respect to your teacher or trainer. But please don't do this bow for me—do it for yourself! You worked hard today and I'm proud of you!

Reverence *(continued)*

Lift up high through your hips and legs and pull your stomach in tight. Take a breath in, bend your standing knee as you move your arms down toward the floor with your upper body. Your front knee is bent, and your back knee stays straight in arabesque.

continues

Slowly lift your body back up as you
straighten your knee and port de bras the
arms back to third position. Change sides and
repeat.

This 60-minute Classic Ballet Beautiful Workout targets all areas of your body and even incorporates some cardio. You can do the workout all at once, or in sections. As you will see in the next chapter, you have many more options for doing single 15-minute workouts, 30-minute combinations, or more challenging 45-minute or 60-minute versions. Onward!

Chapter 6

15-Minute
Ballet Beautiful Blasts!

This chapter introduces my Ballet Beautiful Blasts with Cardio Series in four highly focused and challenging 15-minute programs that will get your heart rate up as you target and transform your arms, legs, abs, and butt.

As Clara shared, "I really love the Ballet Beautiful Blasts! When I'm rushed for time, I do just one. If I have more time, I mix and match the workouts to suit my needs. The Blasts are just genius! I've done them everywhere from hotel rooms to outdoors in a park. I love them and want them to keep on coming!"

As with the Classic Workout, each one of these Ballet Beautiful Blasts targets and defines lean ballet muscles, offering whole-body conditioning—with cardio too! This is a really fun standing workout that makes you look and feel beautiful. My standing work is terrific for strengthening and improving your posture and your center of balance. It is a challenging, comprehensive workout that gets your heart rate up with very little impact and achieves great results.

Think of these exercises as steps in a ballet class. Each one has an important purpose and specific role in transforming and expressing movement in the body, and they can all be woven together to tell a beautiful story. The Blast Series offers options to accompany a longer workout such as the Classic, or you can use them to alternate individual movements in the Classic. It's all up to you! If you find that making room in your schedule for a full hour is impossible, this is the workout for you! I designed the Blasts to be flexible, interchangeable, and high-impact.

You can do the Blasts as single workouts when you are short on time, combine them into a powerful 30- or 60-minute workout, or split them into segments—do one 15-minute workout in the morning and another in the afternoon or evening, depending on your availability. The Blasts are portable—you can do them anywhere—and they incorporate all the principles of the longer series and the program itself: flexibility, balance, posture, and grace. And as you saw in the section on goal setting in Chapter 2, doing a 60-minute workout three times a week can give you major results!

Even if you only have 15 minutes a day to work out, you will still see incredible changes. When you are able to make more time, your results will be even more noticeable and exciting! I believe that every little bit makes a difference when it comes to taking care of your body. I encourage you to squeeze in one of the Blast workouts on days when you may not have more time to stay connected with the program and your goals.

The Blast Series includes four 15-minute Ballet Beautiful workouts:

- Swan Arms
- Cardio Body Blast
- Plié Workout
- Arabesque Workout

Remember to refer to your Ballet Beautiful Principles as you move through the Blast exercises. They will ground your alignment and help you stay in position.

Swan Arms™ Series

The Ballet Beautiful Swan Arms Series is a graceful workout that tones and sculpts lean, feminine arms while building upper body strength and posture. You won't use any weights, and once you try it you will understand why you don't need them—this is a challenging workout that uses the body's own weight to transform the arms and upper body. You can practice your Swan Arms anytime, anywhere, so get ready to have fun!

We will get started with some standing stretches.

Standing Stretch for Legs

Standing Stretch for Legs (see page 58). Bend your right leg in and grab the top of your foot with your right hand, pulling your foot up toward your butt and opening up through the front of your hip and thigh. For balance, pull in through your center or hold on to the wall or a chair for balance.

Change legs and repeat.

Now extend your right leg front and bend your body forward over your front leg in a tendu, keeping your knee straight. Pulse and release through the back of your leg and hamstring. Come up and change legs.

Standing Stretch for Arms

Repeat the stretch on page 57. While standing, lift both arms up to fifth position, keeping your shoulders down and your neck long. Now extend your arms in a port de bras in fourth position, lifting up and over as you bend to the side. From fourth position, extend your top arm slightly back, opening through the chest. Bring your arms down to first position and repeat on the other side.

WHY I LOVE SWAN ARMS!

Swan Lake is one of my all-time favorite ballets. I love the music, the romantic story, and of course the classic choreography. Now that I am no longer performing every day, I also love the way my Swan Arms exercises let me connect with the beauty of ballet while I get a great workout!

Classic Swan Arms

STARTING POSITION: Stand with your neck and shoulders as relaxed as possible, your feet in either first (heels together, toes pointed out) or sixth position (feet parallel), and your knees slightly bent. Remember to keep yourself lifted, but not stiff. Your hands should remain graceful and relaxed; let them simply follow the movement of your arms.

✳ **/ B.** Beginners, take an extra Standing Stretch for the upper body between sets and do 3 rather than 4 sets of 8.

a Pull in through your stomach and open your chest.

b Keep your neck long and stretch your arms out to the side, into second position.

c Drop and bend your elbows down without collapsing your chest—keep your chest open and lifted.

d Lower your arms, then lift your elbows and raise your arms from the elbow, lifting your hands to your shoulders. You can begin slowly and add more speed as you become more comfortable with the movement.

e Lower your arms again and lift, staying lifted and open through your center and chest. Imagine that you are moving through water—have fun! *8 counts, 4 sets.*

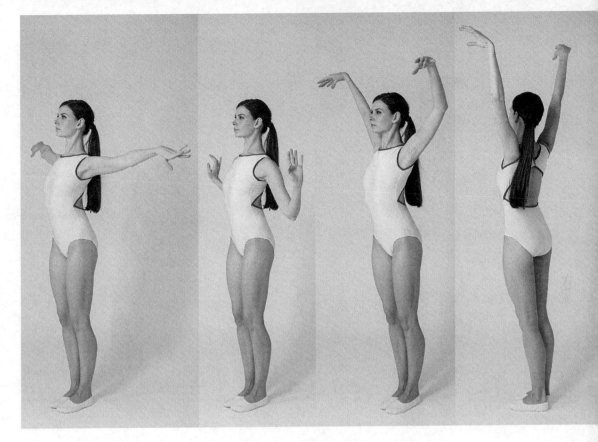

Swan Arms High

a Begin with your arms in the high position: lifted up to your shoulders in second position. Your palms are facing down. Raise your arms up over your shoulders, with your elbows lifting and your neck long. Lift your arms up into a high V position, keeping your palms facing down.

b As you extend your arms out high, stretch all the way through your fingers, then drop your elbows and lower your arms back down to second position.

c Lift your arms again to second position, the high position, beginning with a lift in your elbows and lower side and keeping your neck long and your center engaged. *8 counts, 4 sets.*

* **/B.** Beginners may do an upper body stretch for the arms (the same as the Standing Stretch).

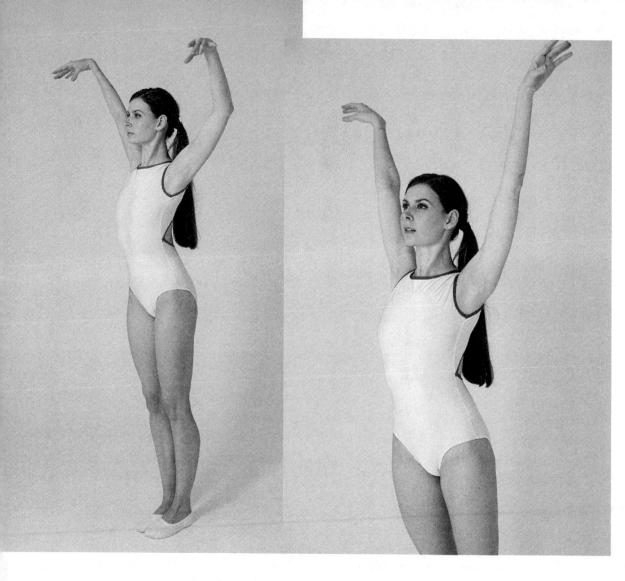

Swan Arms High Pulse

a Hold your arms up in the Swan Arms high position, bend your elbows slightly, then push up and out, stretching all the way through the lines of your arms, from the shoulder through the fingertips!

b Keep your chest open, your neck long, and your stomach engaged.

c Lightly bend then stretch your elbows as you extend long through your arms. *8 counts, 4 sets.*

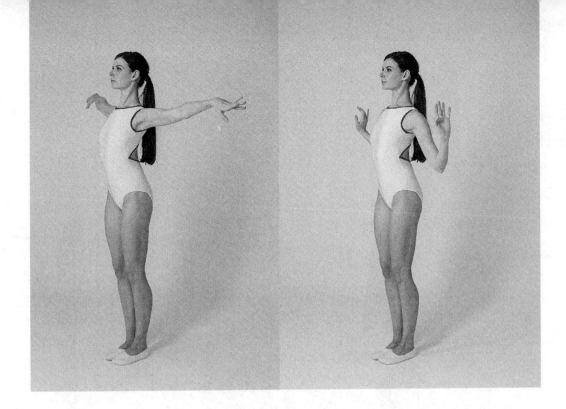

Swan Arms Side

This is a variation on the Classic Swan Arms with less movement in the arms and shoulders. It's a great exercise that lets you stretch long through the muscles in your arms while also providing what I call a "working rest." This exercise gives you a chance to catch your breath and stretch out the muscles as you use them.

a Begin with your arms extended out to second position.

b Next, bend your elbows and bring your hands in toward your shoulders, keeping your neck long and your chest very open.

c Now extend your arms again straight side to second position, stretching long through your joints.

d Repeat, bending and stretching your elbows as you go. Don't hyperextend or lock your elbows; instead, think of pushing through water.

e Keep your chest open, your neck long, and your stomach engaged. *8 counts, 4 sets.*

✴ Remember, these exercises are not just working your arms—they are strengthening your center and improving your posture too! So keep your neck long and your abs pulled in tight through this series. While lifting through your chest and pushing down with your arms, allow these exercises to truly transform you by envisioning yourself in your most graceful and elegant state.

continues

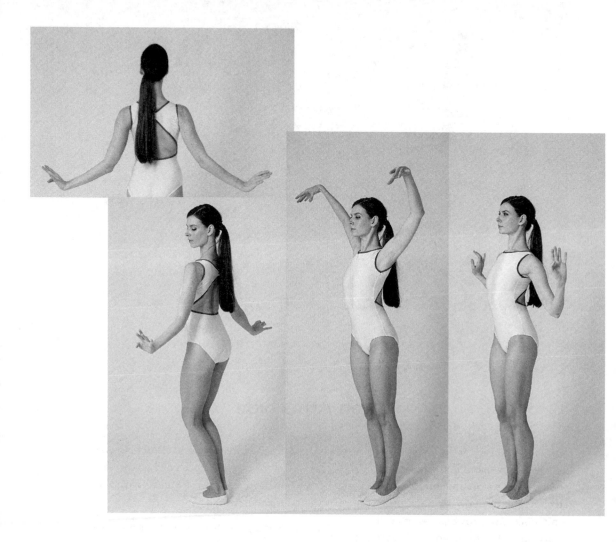

Swan Arms Side (continued)

Stretch: While standing, lift both arms up to fifth position, keeping your shoulders down and your neck long. Now lift your arms into another port de bras to fourth position, lifting up and over as you bend to the side. From fourth position, extend your top arm slightly back, opening through the chest. Bring your arms down to first position and repeat on the other side.

Bring your arms out to second position and repeat another set of Classic Swan Arms, dropping your elbows as you lower your arms and lifting your elbows as you raise them. *8 counts, 4 sets.*

✳ **/B.** Optional stretch for beginners.

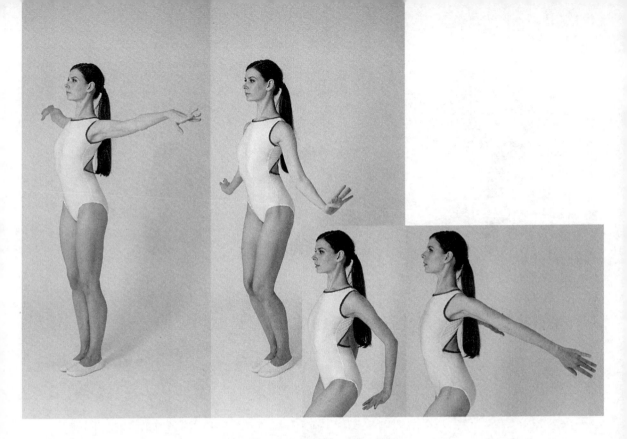

Swan Arms Back

a Begin with your arms extended to the side in second position.

b Drop your elbows and lower your arms to the side and then back as you move your arms behind your hips.

c Your arms are dropping down low here, beneath your hips as you push back with your palms, keeping your chest open.

d Now push out and back with your hands and arms behind your hips and legs, stretching your elbows all the way and extending your arms long behind you.

e Open through the chest and keep your center engaged as you bend your elbows

in and circle your arms back, making sure to stretch your elbows all the way as they push back.

f Circle your arms up and lift them back to second position, lifting with your elbows, stretching your arms, and then dropping your elbows as you lower your arms down to the side and behind your hips, repeating the same motion. Imagine that your arms are under water as you lower them and push them back behind you, opening through the chest and keeping your neck long as you extend. *8 counts, 4 sets.*

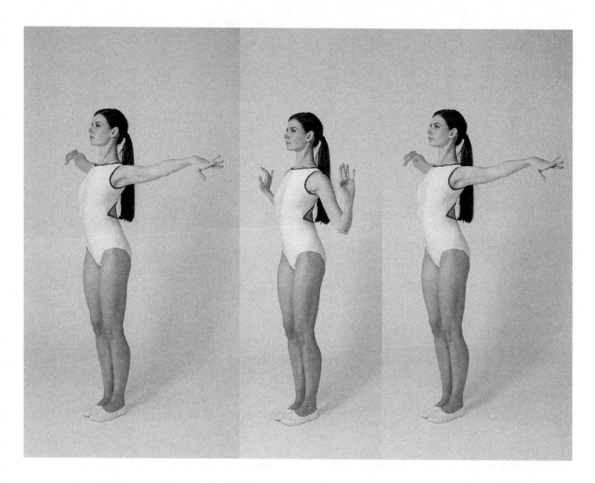

Swan Arms Side—Repeated

With your arms extended into second position and elbows bent in, push your arms straight out to the side, bending and stretching your elbows as you go. Remember not to hyperextend or lock your elbows as you stretch long through the arms. Keep your chest open, your neck long, and your stomach engaged. *8 counts, 4 sets.*

Stretch: Repeat the Standing Stretch on page 123.

Classic Swan Arms—Repeated

a With your arms stretched out to the side and in second position, drop and bend your elbows without collapsing your chest.

b Lower your arms, then lift your elbows and raise your arms from the elbows, lifting your hands to your shoulders.

c Lower your arms again and lift, staying lifted through your center and open through your chest. *8 counts, 4 sets.*

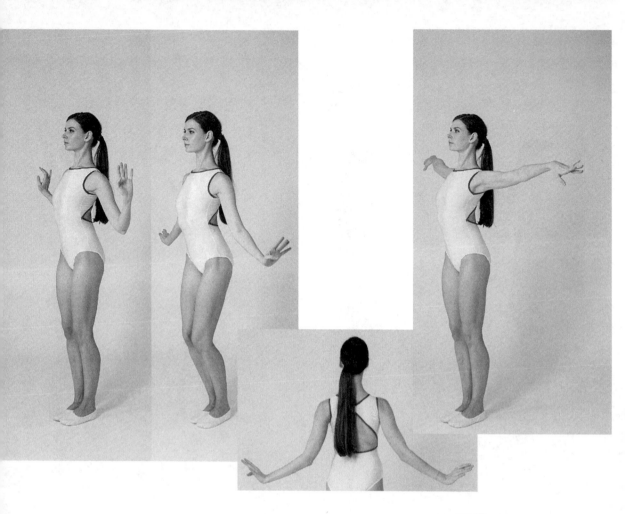

Swan Arms Low

This exercise is like Swan Arms High, but with the arms low beneath the hips.

We will begin in the same starting position as Classic Swan Arms—arms stretched out to second position.

a Now drop your elbows toward your side, with your palms facing down as you lower your arms down toward your legs.

b Stretch your elbows as you extend your arms out to the side, keeping them beneath your hips. Imagine that you are wearing a tulle skirt with lots of layers—this is the distance that you keep your arms from your legs.

c From this low extended position, lift your arms back to second position before bending your elbows, dropping your arms, and repeating the sequence.

d Keep your neck long, your chest open, and your center engaged. *8 counts, 4 sets.*

Swan Arms Low Pulse

a Hold your arms in the Swan Arms Low position, keeping your perfect ballet posture. Push down and stretch out long through your elbows and stretch all the way through to your fingertips!

b Instead of lifting the arms up to second position here, take a slight bend in your elbows, keeping your arms low, and stretch your arms out, again opening through the chest and extending through the elbows. Keep your stomach engaged. *8 counts, 4 sets.*

✳ *IA.* Add a plié with the right leg back to work the legs a bit more deeply.

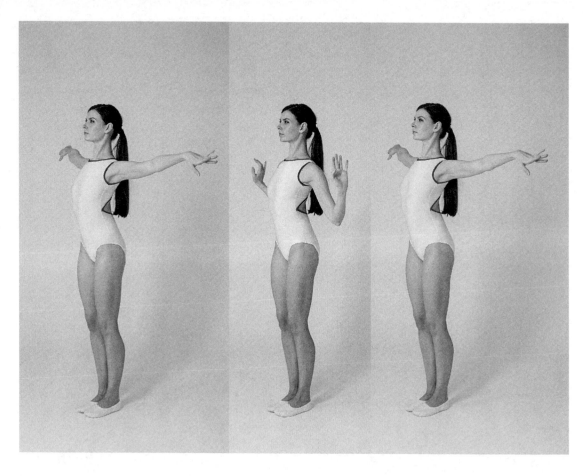

Swan Arms Side—Repeated

Push your arms straight out to the side, bending and stretching your elbows as you go, remembering not to hyperextend or lock them. Keep your chest open, your neck long, and your stomach engaged. Stretch your arms long to finish. *8 counts, 4 sets.*

Stretch: Repeat the Standing Stretch on page 123.

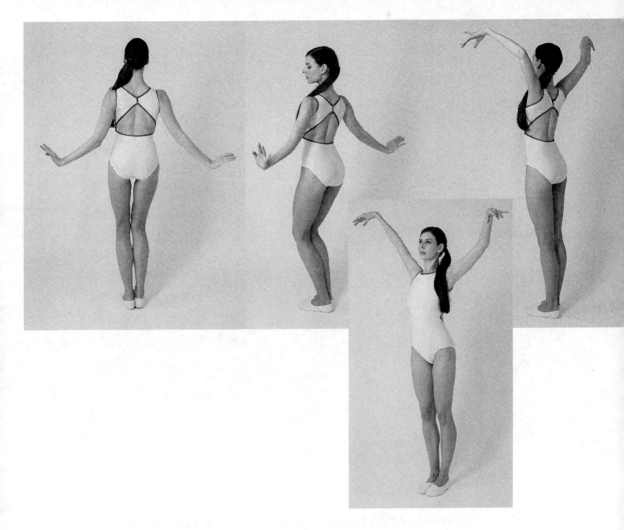

Classic Swan Arms—Repeated

a Lower your arms all the way down to Swan Arms Low position, bending your elbows.

b Lift your elbows, bringing your arms up to shoulder height with your hands lower than your elbows.

c Drop your elbows again and lower your arms down as you open your chest.

d Raise your elbows again as you lift your arms through second position to the height of your shoulders; then lower your arms again, elbows first.

e Keep your neck long and your stomach engaged. Do not tense your neck. *8 counts, 4 sets.*

✳ Stretching here is optional.

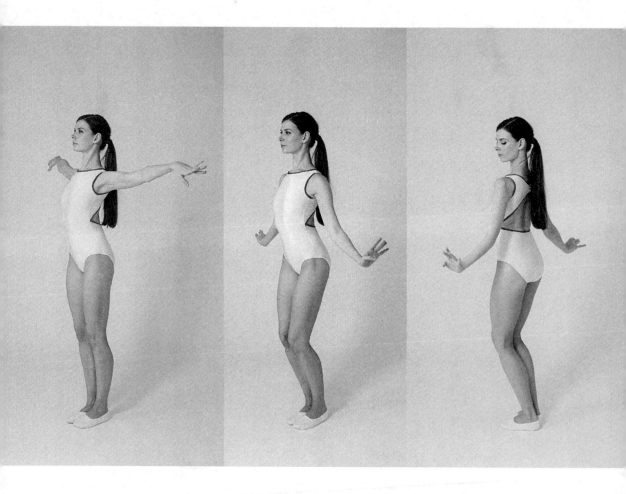

Swan Arms Complete—Low to High

a Begin with your arms in second position, as with Classic Swan Arms. Drop your elbows and lower your arms all the way down to the Swan Arms Low position.

b Lift your elbows and raise your arms high above your shoulders to the Swan Arms High position.

c Drop your elbows and lower your arms back to the Swan Arms Low position, with your stomach engaged and your chest open. Create resistance with your arms by imagining that you are pushing your arms through water or layers of tulle.

d Lift your elbows and raise your arms again to the Swan Arms High position. *8 counts, 4 sets.*

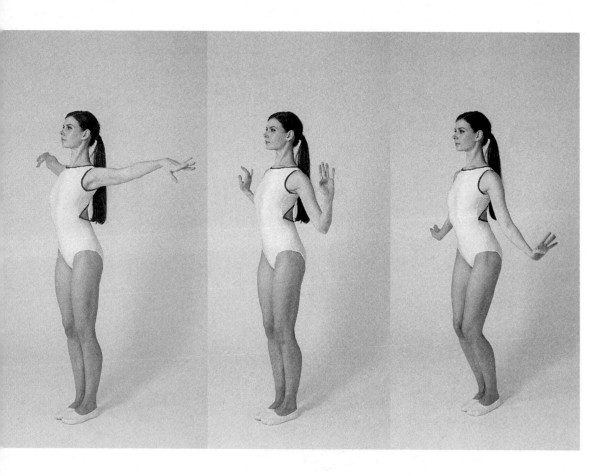

Swan Arms Side–Repeated

Push your arms straight out to the side, bending and stretching your elbows as you go. Don't hyperextend or lock your elbows but imagine you're pushing through water. Keep your chest open, your neck long, and your stomach engaged. Stretch your arms long to finish. *8 counts, 4 sets.*

Stretch: Repeat the Standing Stretch for Arms on page 123.

Cardio Series Body Blast

This Standing Series offers a ballet-inspired full-body workout that's challenging and transformative—and also a lot of fun! My clients always tell me that they love how beautiful these exercises make them feel. If you have only 15 minutes to work out a week, this is the one for you! This workout is one of my favorites before I hit the beach or have a special event. It's a quick, super-effective way to tone and sculpt the body, and it makes you feel elegant too!

We begin the workout with Standing Stretches for the Arms and Legs before taking the starting position.

Standing Stretch for Legs

a Bend your right leg in and grab the top of your foot with your right hand, pulling your foot up toward your butt and opening up through the front of your hip and thigh. For balance, pull in through your center or hold on to a wall or a chair.

b Change legs and repeat.

c Now extend your right leg front and bend your body forward over your front leg in a tendu, keeping your knee straight. Pulse and release through the back of your leg and hamstring. Come up and change legs.

Standing Stretch for Arms

a While standing, lift both arms up to fifth position, keeping your shoulders down and your neck long.

b Now extend your arms in a port de bras in fourth position, lifting up and over as you bend to the side. From fourth position,

extend your top arm slightly back, opening through the chest.

c Bring your arms down to first position and repeat on the other side.

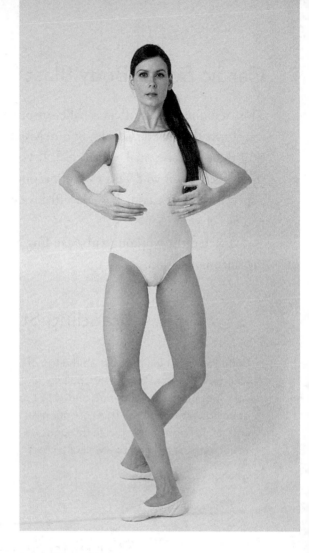

STARTING POSITION: Begin with your arms curved in front of you in first position and your feet in fourth position (feet turned out, about a foot apart).

✳ **/B.** If you are a beginner, your front heel should be in line with the instep of your back foot; **/A.** if you are advanced, line up the heel of your front foot with the toe of your back foot and keep your weight even over both feet.

Pull in tight through your center, keep your neck long, and do not let your elbows droop. Remember the Ballet Beautiful principle about working within your range of motion—be certain that when you bend your knees into a plié they are right over your toes.

Demi-Plié in Fourth Position

a Find a good starting position with your legs in fourth position, one foot in front of the other, and your weight right in the center, equally distributed between your legs.

b Take a demi-plié—a slow bend in your knees—making certain that your knees are over your toes and that your heels remain on the floor.

c Keep your chest open, your neck long, and your center engaged. Do not drop your chest as you plié—stay lifted through your upper body.

d Pulse in a plié, bending your knees a little deeper and stretching up slightly. You should feel this in your inner thighs, hamstrings, and butt. *8 counts, 4 sets.*

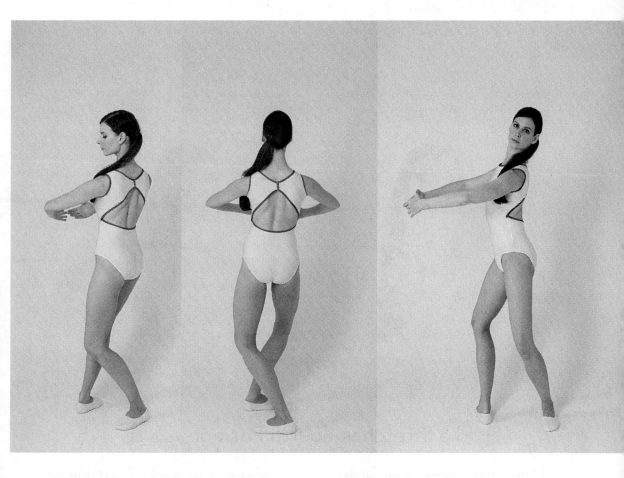

Plié Stretch in Fourth Position

a From the demi-plié position, fully stretch both knees, engaging your inner thighs while your feet remain in fourth position. Keep your arms in first position, curved in front of you.

b Bend your knees again into a plié, as in Demi-Plié in Fourth Position, then stretch all the way straight without shifting your feet. Keep your weight right between your legs. This time extend your arms open to the sides to second position as you stretch through your legs and knees.

c Keep the "work within your range of motion" principle in mind here—be careful not to overrotate your feet and keep your knees over your toes when you plié. Remember that your feet may not open as wide as mine.

continues

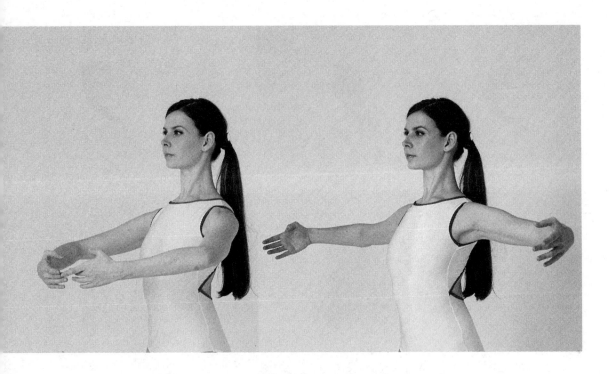

Plié Stretch in Fourth Position *(continued)*

d Stretch through your legs and lift your kneecaps all the way each time you straighten and lift, this time with the arms in first position. Alternate your arms between first and second position each time you stretch your knees, and remain in first position for each plié.

e Keep your chest open and your stomach engaged. *8 counts, 4 sets.*

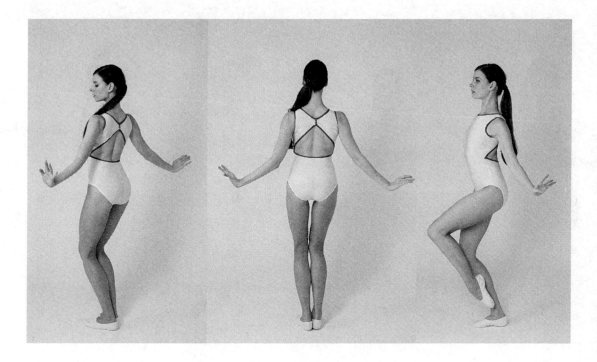

Plié Pulse in Parallel

a Bring your feet together to sixth position. (Imagine your feet in first position, heels together, toes open, then close your toes together, taking a parallel position, heels together.)

b Lift your right foot slightly off the floor into a coupé and bend the standing knee (your left knee).

c Open your chest and arms into a Swan Arms Low position, pulling your stomach in tight and keeping your neck long.

d Pulse here in a plié, keeping your core steady and lifted.

* **/B.** If you are a beginner and are having difficulty with your balance, you may hold on to a wall or a chair as a makeshift barre. Another option for extra stability is to keep the toes of the foot in coupé touching the floor. *8 counts, 4 sets.*

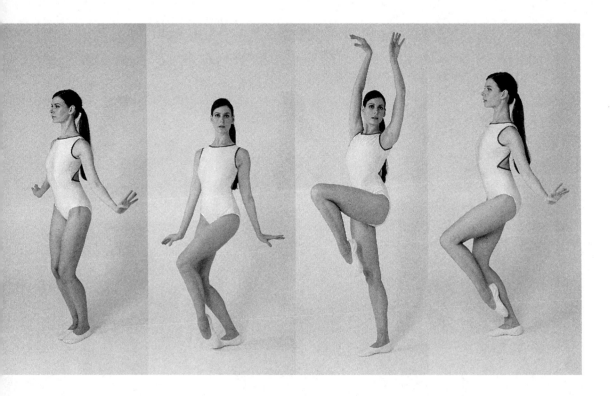

Passé Lift in Parallel

a Bring your feet together to sixth position. (Imagine your feet in first position, heels together, toes open, then close your toes together, taking a parallel position, heels together.)

b Lift one foot slightly off the floor, pointing the toe into a coupé position and bending the standing knee.

c Open your chest and arms into a Swan Arms Low position.

d Stretch the standing knee and lift your leg into a passé parallel as you lift your arms up high above your head, bringing your wrists toward each other, with your palms facing out. Your right foot should slide up your left leg from the ankle to the kneecap. Bend and stretch the knee fully.

e Keep your stomach in and your chest open. Engage your center. *8 counts, 4 sets.*

f Repeat steps a through d on the other side.

Stretch: Standing Stretch for Legs.

Putting It Together into a Ballet Step: The Pirouette!

Have you ever wondered what a pirouette is? It's a turn that literally means "to whirl about." The classic ballet pirouette starts in a plié in fourth position, just as in this exercise. In the Balanchine style, your weight would be on your front foot and your back leg would be extended out straight behind you in what I call a ballet lunge. As a New York City Ballet dancer, this is my favorite style and preferred position to turn from!

If you are turning to the right, your right leg would be back. From here you would extend the same arm (your right arm) out long in front and open your left arm to second position. Pulling in tight through your stomach, push off with all of your weight front as you lift your back leg into a passé (foot to the knee, leg turned out) and turn. Lots of fun!

Attitude Lift

If you have ever seen the ballet version of *Sleeping Beauty*, you know how classic and beautiful an attitude is as a ballet step! There is a famous scene in Aurora's pas de deux where she balances in attitude en pointe for what seems like forever as her suitors promenade her in the court. It's a beautiful and suspenseful scene to watch, and executing it takes incredible balance and perfect form! In a proper attitude, the standing knee should be very straight, and the knee lifted into the air in attitude back

should be bent with the knee at about 90 degrees, The upper body must stay relaxed.

a Start in a plié in fourth position, with your arms in first position. Keep your knees over your toes and your chest open. From this plié you are going to lift your back leg up into the air in an attitude—an extension back with the knee bent.

b Pull your stomach in and lift your arms up to fifth position (curved high above your head) as you lift up your back leg and

stretch the standing knee. Be certain to engage your center as you lift—this will prevent you from arching your back.

c Lower your foot back to fourth position, taking care not to drop your chest. Bring your arms down to first position, curved in front of you, and keep your weight on your front foot.

d Lift again and repeat. *8 counts, 4 sets.*

✻ **/B.** Beginners can take an extra Standing Stretch for Legs here and work with just 2 or 3 sets of 8.

Attitude Plié Pulse

a From the attitude position in Attitude Lift—with your back leg raised and bent—bend your front knee and open your arms out to the side to second position.

b Keep your chest open and your stomach in.

c Pulse here in plié, staying relaxed through your upper body. Keep your back leg stretched and elevated. *8 counts, 4 sets.*

Stretch: Standing Stretch for Legs.

Change legs and repeat Plié Pulse in Parallel, Passé Lift in Parallel, Attitude Lift, and Attitude Plié Pulse on the other side.

Standing Abs

These standing exercises for your abs and obliques use a beautiful port de bras to sculpt and define your waist while also improving your center of balance.

a Begin with your feet in fourth position. Bend your knees into a plié and extend your right leg back straight into tendu arabesque. Make sure your weight is over your front foot. You can test this by lifting your back leg up off the floor—if your upper body moves forward when you do this, your weight is back. Adjust accordingly.

b Lift your left arm (the opposite arm from the extended leg) up and over into fourth position, pulling in with your stomach.

c Keep your weight over your front foot and really bend with your torso, lifting up and over with your arms.

d Extend through your arms and lift up and open to second position as you straighten your front leg. Stretching this knee changes the movement from tendu plié to a tendu with straight knees—it's also great for the butt and leg!

continues

Standing Abs *(continued)*

e Take a breath and lift and bend your arms back into another port de bras in fourth position to the right side, bending your front knee into plié as you do so. Pull in again through your stomach, keep your weight over your front leg, and really bend with your upper body. Now straighten the standing leg again as you lift your arms to second position.

f Keep pulling in through your stomach the entire time and really stretch and bend your standing knee and upper body to fully engage the muscles through your center and side. *8 counts, 4 sets.*

Standing Ab Pulse

a Begin from the extended position in Standing Abs, with your knee in demi-plié and your arms in fourth position.

b Pull in with your stomach and pulse your arms to the side, lifting and bending your upper body to the side with your legs in a lunge position. *8 counts, 4 sets.*

c Change sides and repeat on the other side.

Standing Ab Twist

a Begin in the same starting position as in Standing Abs: legs in fourth position, knees bent into a plié, and right leg extended back straight into tendu arabesque.

b With your chest open and your stomach in, lift your arms to first position.

c Pull in your stomach as you rotate to the side, twisting your upper body toward your front knee.

d Keep your legs and hips still as you twist, extending your arms long to fourth arabesque. Both arms are straight here, and the upper body twists as you pull in through your center and abs.

e Pivot back to the starting position with your arms returning to first position and your torso facing front, without changing your legs. *8 counts, 4 sets.*

Ab Twist in a Lunge with a Pulse

a Hold in the extended position of the second part of the Standing Ab Twist.

b Pull your stomach in tight and pulse in a twist. Keep your shoulders relaxed and your knee over your toes. You should feel the muscles through your center and sides engaging here. *8 counts, 4 sets.*

Stretch: Standing Stretch for Arms and Legs.

Repeat Standing Abs, Standing Ab Pulse, Standing Ab Twist, and Ab Twist in a Lunge with a Pulse on the other side.

Cardio Series: Plié Workout

A plié is the most basic of ballet positions—it's the starting point for any turn, jump, or waltz, not to mention the first exercise in the warm-up at the barre each day in ballet class. It also makes for an incredible workout for your legs, butt, and abs. A plié lets you connect with the ground and work a wide range of muscles. It's the starting point for many more difficult steps and moves!

Those of you who are just beginning may feel a bit awkward doing pliés, so give yourself some time. In a couple of weeks, you will be doing this graceful, ballet-inspired move with ease!

If you are moving directly from one of the other Blasts and have just stretched out, you can skip the stretch here. If you are starting cold, do a Standing Stretch for the Arms and Legs before transitioning into the starting position.

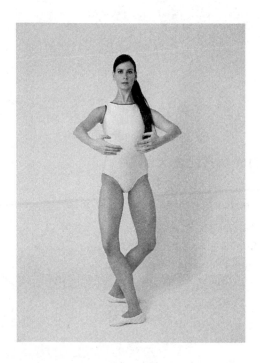 

STARTING POSITION: We will begin our plié workout with the feet in fourth position, weight evenly distributed between the legs, arms in first position, knees over toes, and chest open.

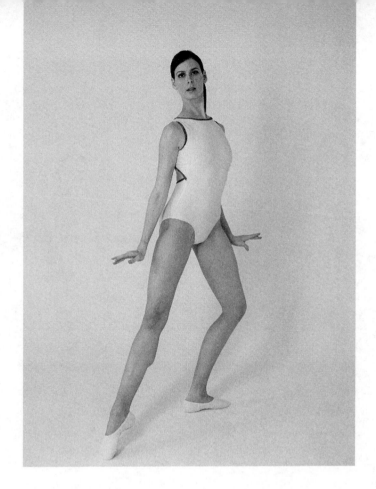

Plié Tendu Side

a From your plié in fourth position, rond de jambe (circle) your back leg to second position with your knee straight into tendu side. The standing knee remains slightly bent in a demi-plié, and the right leg is extended to the side to second position. Arms are in the Swan Arms Low position.

b Keep your chest open and your stomach pulled flat.

c Bend the standing knee slightly deeper and slide the extended leg out along the floor. Stretch the standing knee, pulling up

straight, then bend into a plié again. The right knee is extended straight in tendu the entire time here.

d Make sure your standing knee is over your left toe. Keep your chest open, your elbows lifted, and your center engaged.

e Pulse here in plié tendu. *8 counts, 4 sets.*

✳ **/B.** If you are just getting started, hold on to a chair or the wall for extra stability. And don't forget to take a moment for an extra stretch as you go!

Plié Tendu with Straight Knee

a Extend down deep into a tendu plié, as in Plié Tendu Side, but in Swan Arms Low position.

b Now straighten the standing knee, pulling in through your stomach and lifting up with both knees straight. Lift the arms into Swan Arms High position as you straighten the standing knee, and keep your neck long.

c Bend the standing knee again into a plié and extend your arms back to Swan Arms Low; then straighten again and lower your arms back to second position.

d Engage your center, butt, and inner thighs. Be careful not to collapse your upper body when you bend your knees in demi-plié. Your gaze should be straight forward, not at the ground. *8 counts, 4 sets.*

Plié Tendu with a Hold

a Resume the starting position in Plié Tendu with Straight Knee—a plié tendu side with Swan Arms High.

b Check your form: standing knee over toes, stomach pulled in, chest open, arms extending to the side.

c Hold here in plié. *8 counts, 4 sets.*

Stretch: Standing Stretch for Legs.

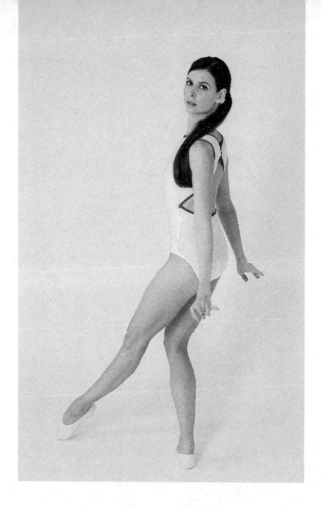

Plié Tendu Front

a Rond de jambe (circle) your leg in tendu side to a tendu front, with your arms lowered to the side and slightly back. Keep your stomach engaged and your chest open.

b Bend the standing knee into a plié and then bend slightly deeper in plié. Keep your front leg extended into a tendu front and arms in Swan Arms Back.

c Bend the standing knee slightly deeper and slide the extended leg out along the floor. Stretch the standing knee, pulling up slightly; then bend into a plié again. Your working knee is extended straight in tendu the entire time here.

d Make sure your standing knee is over your toes. Keep your chest open, your elbows lifted, and your center engaged.

e Pulse here in plié tendu. *8 counts, 4 sets.*

Plié Tendu Front with Straight Knee

a Begin with the starting position for Plié Tendu Front. With your arms in Swan Arms Back position, bend the standing knee into a demi-plié, keeping your heel on the ground, and then stretch the standing leg, lifting with your knee as you lift your arms to Swan Arms High position. Keep your front leg extended into a tendu front.

b Bend the standing knee into another plié. Keep your chest open and your stomach pulled in as you lower your arms to Swan Arms Back. *8 counts, 4 sets.*

c Straighten again and lift your arms up to Swan Arms High position.

d Repeat, remembering to engage your center, butt, and inner thighs. Be careful not to collapse your upper body when you bend. *8 counts, 4 sets.*

Plié Tendu Front with a Hold

a Extend into a plié tendu front, as in Plié Tendu Front with Straight Knee, with your arms in Swan Arms Low position.

b Check your form: stomach pulled in, chest open, standing knee over toe.

c Hold here. *8 counts, 4 sets.*

Stretch: Standing Stretch for Legs.

Plié Tendu Arabesque

a From the front, rond de jamb (circle) your right leg back, moving your leg from your hip. Imagine your toe drawing a half-circle on the floor. Be sure to keep your leg quiet and focus on the movement from your hip. Your arms are in Swan Arms Back here— down to the sides and behind your hips. Your stomach is engaged and your chest open. Do not arch your back.

b Pulse here in a plié arabesque. *8 counts, 4 sets.*

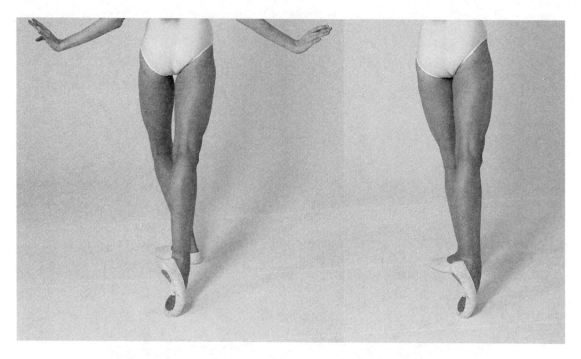

Plié Tendu Arabesque with Straight Knee

a From the starting position in plié tendu arabesque, move from a demi-plié with your arms in Swan Arms Back to a straight standing knee as your arms lift to second position.

b Bend the standing knee again to demi-plié and lower your arms, keeping your back leg extended into tendu arabesque. Lift your arms back to second position, pulling in through the stomach and opening through the chest as you stretch the standing knee. *8 counts, 4 sets.*

Plié Tendu Arabesque with a Hold

a Return to your plié tendu arabesque back, with your arms in Swan Arms Back. Check your placement—standing knee over your toe, stomach engaged, chest open.

b Hold here in a demi-plié. *8 counts, 4 sets.*

Stretch: Standing Stretch for Arms and Legs.

Change legs and repeat the nine movements of the Plié Workout on the other side.

The Arabesque Workout

An arabesque is one of the most classic ballet steps! It also provides a fantastic workout that tones your legs, butt, back, center, and upper body.

We will get started with a quick Standing Stretch for the Arms and Legs.

STARTING POSITION: Begin standing up tall, with your chest open, your stomach pulled in, your feet in fourth position, and your arms in second position. Extend your back leg into a tendu, keeping your front leg bent in a ballet lunge.

Warm-up with a Plié Pulse in Fourth Position

a From your ballet lunge in fourth position, drop your arms down with a slight bend in your elbows to the Swan Arms Low position.

b Bend your front knee into a demi-plié and make certain that your knee is over your toes and your back leg is straight. Your back toe should be on the ground and your heel slightly lifted.

c Keep your chest open, your neck long, and your center engaged.

d Pulse in a plié here, bending your knee a little deeper and stretching. As you deepen the plié on the standing leg, drop the back heel to the floor. *8 counts, 4 sets.*

✳ **/B.** Beginners can hold on to a wall or a chair for extra stability. Even the kitchen counter will work! Use stretches between reps to give your muscles a chance to recover, and remember that you can begin working with fewer reps and increase the difficulty over time.

Stretch: Standing Stretch for Upper Body and Legs.

Tendu in Arabesque with a Plié Pulse

a From the same starting position as Warm-up with a Plié Pulse in Fourth Position, bend your front knee into a ballet lunge and extend your other leg straight behind you, this time pointing your toe into a tendu back. The weight is over your front foot.

b Lift your arms to first position, pulling your stomach in tight. Your chest is very open, and your elbows are lifted.

c Bend your knee a bit more and extend further down into a deeper plié.

d Keep your chest very open and lifted. Do not collapse as you plié—this is terrific for your posture and back!

e Pulse here in plié. You will feel your standing leg working and your butt and stomach engaging. *8 counts, 4 sets.*

✳ **/B.** Beginners can do 2 sets of 8, followed by Standing Stretch for Legs, then another 2 sets of 8.

Tendu Arabesque with Lift

a From the starting position in Tendu in Arabesque with a Plié Pulse, bend your front knee and extend your back leg in tendu. Your arms are in first position, your chest is open, and your stomach is engaged.

b Now lift your back leg up off the floor in arabesque, keeping the standing knee bent. Lift your arms to second position.

c While stretching your back knee straight behind you, keep pulling in through your stomach and don't arch your back.

d Lower your working leg back to the floor (keeping your foot pointed) and keep your front knee bent. Be careful not to drop your chest as your leg lowers. Stay very lifted through your upper body. Your arms can come back to first position, as above.

e Pull and lift up again into arabesque, raising your arms to second position and keeping the standing knee bent. *8 counts, 4 sets.*

* A chair or wall makes a great makeshift ballet barre, so feel free to hold on to one or the other for support if needed. Also, don't worry about how high your back leg lifts into arabesque. Keep your back knee straight and your stomach engaged. Your leg will lift higher in time.

Tendu Arabesque Lift with Straight Leg

This one really targets the muscles in your legs, back, and butt!

a The starting position is going to change slightly here. Extend your arms into Swan Arms Low while keeping your back leg extending into an arabesque tendu on the ground, with your standing knee bent into a demi-plié.

b Pull your stomach in and lift through your inner thighs.

c Relax through the upper body and move the arms into first arabesque.

d Now lift your back leg up off the floor, keeping your stomach in and your front knee straight, taking care not to arch your back as you stretch the standing knee.

e Lower your arms slightly as you lower your back leg down to a tendu on the floor and lift again. Keep both knees straight throughout this exercise. *8 counts, 4 sets.*

Arabesque Lift with Straight Leg High

a From the starting position for Tendu Arabesque Lift with Straight Leg, a tendu arabesque, lift your back leg into the air (keeping your front leg straight). Keep pulling in and engaging your stomach, and do not arch your back as you lift your leg.

b Keep both knees straight and both arms straight in fourth position. Keep your stomach pulled in and your chest open.

c Lift your leg up slightly higher.

Then lower it slightly, keeping it in the air the entire time. *8 counts, 4 sets.*

✳ Remember that your back leg doesn't need to lift very high when you are getting started. I would prefer that you keep your back leg lower and stay engaged through your center and abs as you lift into arabesque back. As you gain strength and flexibility, you'll be able to take your back leg up a little in the air.

Arabesque High with Plié

a From the starting position in Arabesque Lift with Straight Leg High, lift your back leg into arabesque and then bend the standing knee into a plié. Extend your arm (on the same side as the elevated leg) to the side and lift your other arm up above your head into third position (your standing arm curved above your head, your working arm out to the side, at shoulder height).

b Keep your back knee straight in arabesque, your stomach pulled in, and your chest open.

c Bend the standing knee slightly deeper and pulse here in a plié with your back leg extended, arms extended as in step **a**. *8 counts, 4 sets.*

Arabesque High with Plié Stretch

This is a variation of the Arabesque Lift with Straight Leg High and the Arabesque High with Plié that works more deeply through the back of the leg and inner thigh.

a Begin as in the Arabesque High with Plié, with your arms in third position.

b Now pull your stomach in and stretch the standing knee into a lifted arabesque position, with both knees straight and your back leg in the air. Remember to keep your working leg stretched out long behind you and pull in with your stomach to engage your center and protect your back.

c Straighten both arms into first arabesque and pull your stomach in tight as you stretch the standing knee.

d Bend the standing knee again into a plié, bending your top arm back to third position and leaving your other arm in second position at your side. Stretch the standing leg, keeping your back leg in arabesque. Don't arch your back or drop your chest.

e Repeat. *8 counts, 4 sets.*

Stretch: Standing Stretch for Arms and Legs.

If you have extra time, join me on the mat for a Hip Opener and Inner Thigh Stretch.

Change sides and repeat all the movements of the Arabesque Workout except the first one.

These 15-minute Blasts are yours to play with—you can combine them with each other, replace segments in the Classic workout, or do them singly or together.

When you have time to do all four Blasts together, you will get an incredible full-body workout. If you have only 30 minutes to work out, consider the following combinations:

- Cardio Series Body Blast and Swan Arms: A full-body workout with a focus on the arms

- Swan Arms and the Plié Workout, or Swan Arms with the Arabesque Workout: An intense workout for the arms and legs

- Plié Workout combined with the Arabesque Workout: Incredible leg and butt workout that will get your heart rate up

If you want to thank yourself for a good workout, make sure to do a reverence (see the end of the previous chapter). This is also a nice stretch and a fun way to end a workout!

Always remember to stretch and drink water, and equally important—have fun and enjoy your amazing results!

PART III

THE BALLET BEAUTIFUL LIFESTYLE

*The secret to any successful eating plan is satisfaction
—not deprivation.*

Chapter 7

Dieting Is a
Waste of Time

I have a friend who once said to me, "In the time that I wasted thinking about calories, I could have learned Japanese!" She's right. So many of us let calories drive us crazy. We obsess over this or that food—and I bet you know as well as I do that all that comes of obsessing over calories and dieting are misery and weight gain. Food is a necessary part of life, and it's one that we can all learn to embrace and enjoy! And just as with exercise, finding the right balance with nutrition is a wonderful way to enhance your health, nourish your body, and improve the way you look and feel.

You may have heard about ballerinas' crazy diets—grapefruits, cigarettes, and coffee—but you won't find any of those unhealthy extremes here! To perform at your best, whether it's as a professional ballerina, a mom, a businesswoman, an artist, or even a student, you have to nourish and feed your body—and your brain!

In the ballet world, just as in the regular world, women are socialized at a young age to restrict what they eat. There can be pressure to maintain a certain body image, and this emphasis can unwittingly trigger a dangerous, self-denying cycle of bingeing on the wrong foods and thinking of the right foods as off-limits and less than fulfilling. I remember being shocked when I arrived at the School of American Ballet, the official school of the New York City Ballet, and all of the girls were eating frozen yogurt with sprinkles for lunch. (This was the '90s! Fro-yo was all the rage.) I tried it once and was left starving; I had no energy for my afternoon variations class and couldn't concentrate in my lessons at school. Without the protein, fiber, and grains I was used to, my body couldn't function and I was underperforming. I quickly went back to my go-to lunch, a whole-wheat turkey sandwich and fresh fruit.

This chapter is all about rediscovering your natural relationship with eating—yes, it's true and possible! The Ballet Beautiful lifestyle is utterly "anti-diet," and I am convinced that that is why it works! You will see how safe, simple, and easy it is to stop using food as a tool for self-destruction or as a way to pass the time when you are bored.

As Katherine told me, "The key thing that I have learned from Ballet Beautiful is that nothing has to be all one way or another. Ballet Beautiful has helped me get away from the extremes of dieting that I think so many of us have struggled with. I learned to make simple substitutions that go a long way in how I look and feel. These have completely changed my life!"

Jenna's shift in how she thinks about food and nutrition was more subtle: "I was already eating healthfully, but now I'm more aware. I'm not obsessive but aware. I might think twice before eating a cheeseburger, and I am definitely eating healthier snacks—like nuts and fruit—throughout the day."

The word *diet* has a negative association for many of us—it can bring up feelings of failure, anger, and resentment from the past. I feel grouchy and depressed just contemplating the word because that's how dieting made me feel—deprived, food-obsessed, and out of sorts! Ballet Beautiful is a lifestyle, not a diet—and the information in this chapter will help you achieve and maintain a healthy, deprivation-free way of eating that perfectly complements the other parts of the program. It is truly possible to shift the way you think about food, learn to trust yourself to make healthy choices *most* of the time, and reset your natural relationship with food!

The Five Ballet Beautiful Eating Principles

I am grateful to have learned that dieting is not only unnecessary but counterproductive to health and weight loss goals. The extreme measures that allow many of even the most popular diets to take the pounds off fast make failure inevitable because they are not sustainable over a period of time. The roller coaster up and down on the scale from extreme dieting is incredibly damaging to your psyche, your self-esteem, and your overall health. I've been there, and it is rough! But the pattern is also something that can be overcome. So let's ditch the diet thinking and focus instead on how to achieve and maintain your goals through great nutrition with my Five Easy Eating Principles.

1. *Be prepared!*—I always try to organize my shopping so that I have healthy food available in my refrigerator and pantry at all times. When I am on the road or have a long day of training ahead, I make sure to pack healthy snacks. This idea seems so basic, but a lot of healthy eating plans get derailed because hunger strikes—leading us to overeat or make poor food choices.

2. *Eat often!*—This may sound counterintuitive, but I always tell my clients to eat more! To lose weight and speed up your metabolism, you must feed your body the right foods on a fairly regular basis. The question is, what to eat? I'll tell you how to cue into your body so you know when it is hungry and the types of foods to eat to keep your metabolism burning all day long.

3. *Substitute for satisfaction!*—I am against any kind of deprivation whatsoever. Rather than restricting calories or denying yourself foods that you love and enjoy, I advocate finding substitutions—healthier options instead of foods that will make you bloated, tired, and cranky. There's no room for deprivation in Ballet Beautiful.

4. *Be flexible!*—Being flexible is being realistic: not one of us can eat perfectly, work out daily, and keep life from intervening. We work, we have families, vacations, and holidays, and other unexpected events arise and impact us. The key to this principle is staying clear on your goals and relying on strategies that help you adapt your workout and meals to your real life.

5. *Forgive yourself and move on!*—I always tell my clients to forget about yesterday's mistakes and focus on today. A successful healthy eating plan

provides tips to get back on track when you do slip or overindulge. Not every meal can be a healthy one and that's okay—the important thing is learning how to quickly get back on track and not let an unhealthy meal or snack unsettle your inner balance and throw you off your program. A cheeseburger and fries for dinner one night does not mean that you're doomed to eating cheeseburgers and fries at every meal!

Everyone knows that a healthy way of eating is paramount to happiness and the body you want to achieve and inhabit. My Five Easy Eating Principles will help you simplify and streamline how you think about food, teach you how to make healthy food choices, and show you how to maximize and support your new fitness regime. The principles complement the Ballet Beautiful program as a whole because they reflect the same ideals—balance, health, portability, and realistic, attainable goals. Ballet Beautiful will help you whether you want to lose 20 pounds, slim down a size, or maintain a good weight for your body without worrying and obsessing about calories, complicated recipes, or a punishing diet.

This easy-to-follow eating plan is high in nutrition and built around whole, satisfying foods. I designed this balanced program specifically to avoid the inevitable pitfalls and extremes inherent in diets that promise quick weight loss. Your new Ballet Beautiful mindset is a big part of this plan: it will help you set and achieve your weight loss goals—and maintain them for life! You will be able to enjoy your favorite treats without resorting to calorie counting, and you will not be hungry and obsessed with food. The plan easily and fluidly helps you internalize a new balanced lifestyle with a focus on lasting health and happiness.

Together we will focus not on what you *cannot* eat, but rather on what you *can*. You will find easy-to-remember tips on what to put in your shopping cart, as well as recipes for my favorite meals that make this program easy to follow. I won't make you commit to a long list of forbidden foods. Instead, Ballet Beautiful helps you overcome bad habits and encourages you to focus on the positive, opening doors to incredible possibilities and nutritious food groups while providing you with the keys to making a balanced, healthy, and fit life attainable.

Principle 1: Be Prepared!

Life is stressful, chaotic, and unpredictable, and one of the best ways to make good nutrition a part of your daily life is to be prepared. For me this means always keeping healthy food in my fridge, in the cupboards at my studio, or in my bag when I'm traveling so that I don't ever get too hungry. Hunger is one of the first triggers to overeating and making poor food choices. This is true for everyone! No matter how much you know about nutrition, if you are ravenous, it's hard not only to make the right food choices but to know when to stop.

Though there is no one reason that explains why people overeat or lose their ability to feel full or sated, certain biochemical triggers clearly undermine appetite control. When I get too hungry or go too long without eating, I kick into what I call "starvation mode": I am literally ravenous, and this is when I feel vulnerable and can lose control. This is exactly when it's good to reach for a high-protein snack like a boiled egg or Greek yogurt to calm your hunger before you launch into a larger meal.

When our bodies go too long without food, the brain releases chemicals that make us feel hungrier, which in turn make us want to eat. This reaction happens more frequently when we eat foods that are less nutritious, such as starchy carbs, processed foods high in sugar, or fats. But when the body is fed foods that are high in fiber and rich in nutrients, including lean proteins—such as whole grains, fruits, and vegetables—the body is fuller longer and responds less drastically to these signals to eat.

Sometimes life gets in the way and you go too long without food by accident. When this happens, I try to help my body by reaching first for proteins and healthy fats before I move into fiber and carbs to keep myself from (1) overeating and (2) feeling sick. This helps to satisfy me without going overboard.

Sound complicated? It's really not. If you make choices from the Ballet Beautiful healthy whole food lists, you will feel more satisfied, eat more frequently, not crave the sweet stuff, and lose weight. Sound good?

My days are a busy mix of leading classes, filming videos, creating new Ballet Beautiful exercises, going to meetings, and traveling from city to city. The best way to be prepared is to make sure I have easy access to healthy, wholesome foods, no matter how hectic life gets. I keep healthy snacks like fresh fruit and nuts on hand throughout the day to keep me energized and feeling strong. Keeping healthy foods at home for quick, easy meals is also key. Having salad makings, healthy soups, and prepared dinner foods like an organic roast chicken at the ready can help you to avoid the temptation to order in pizza or grab fast food on the drive home after a long day at work. (You will learn more about my "flash cooking" in Chapter 9!)

Learning to anticipate situations that will challenge your health goals is also important. For example, don't assume that you will be able to buy a healthy salad when you are in the airport, or that you will be able to turn down fried appetizers at a cocktail party after work when you are stressed out and starving. Especially if you have a drink and weaken your resolve! Being prepared can mean bringing food with you when you are on the go or eating a healthy snack or light meal before a party or dinner where food is an unknown. I also find it a lot easier to pass up the dessert tray at a party if I know that my favorite dark chocolate is waiting for me at home!

I love dark chocolate and indulge in some almost every day! My current favorite is Green & Black's Dark, either the 70 or 85 percent cacao mix. I bring it to room temperature before I dive in and try to eat it in the afternoon because it sometimes keeps me up at night. It's also delicious with red wine or herbal tea after dinner on nights when I eat early.

While the Ballet Beautiful way of eating emphasizes fresh, whole, unprocessed foods, there are some packaged snacks that I like, such as organic crackers from my local health food store. Another choice would be a nonfat Greek yogurt with fruit and honey or a bowl of fresh fruit or berries in season. I often have a small glass of skimmed or almond milk with dessert at night for extra protein and calcium.

Principle 2: Eat Often!

Rather than focus on when to eat during the day, it's more efficient to simply remember to eat often. What do I mean by "often"? A general rule of thumb is to make sure you eat a meal or a snack every four hours. I'm not saying eat six meals a day—or every hour! A healthy meal or snack every four or so hours will keep you going—you don't have to

BREAKFAST IS A MUST!

I'm sure this isn't the first time you have heard that eating a balanced breakfast is the best way to kick-start a healthy day. But are you actually doing it? I'm always surprised when my clients confess that they have been skipping breakfast and thrilled when they tell me how much better they feel once they change that habit. The right breakfast will do wonders for your energy levels and your waist by keeping you energized and satisfied and your metabolism humming.

The key is finding foods you enjoy that are easy to prepare on days when you are rushed. Muesli with skimmed milk, whole-grain crackers or a piece of whole-wheat toast with peanut butter, a single serving of nonfat Greek yogurt with raw nuts—these are all quick-and-easy breakfasts that will leave you energized and take no time to prepare. I'm not asking you to cook and eat egg whites and asparagus!

survive on mini-meals. The point is to never let yourself get too hungry. We all have different metabolisms.

To keep your body's metabolism humming, you need to give it fuel. Small snacks and light meals throughout the day actually encourage your body to keep metabolizing (burning) food, especially when you feed it healthy, nutritious foods. Eating frequently also helps to maintain your energy. One of the worst triggers for cravings or overeating is letting the body get low in blood sugar.

No single eating plan can work for everyone because each body and life is unique. Some people are grazers and feel best eating many small meals. I really enjoy food and hate being hungry! I feel best eating three to four square meals a day, with healthy snacks, to keep me satisfied and on track.

Breakfast is non-negotiable—an absolute must for any healthy lifestyle. I try to start each day with a healthy breakfast, no matter when I rise. What I eat varies depending on how much time I have, so I keep lots of options handy. My approach to nutrition and diet is that it needs to be sustainable over a lifetime, not just until you get into a summer bikini or a dress for a big holiday event. I find that this attitude about food and eating keeps my weight consistent and prevents the wide fluctuation in numbers that I used to see on the scale.

As you will see in the menu plans in the pages ahead, you can time your snacks and meals in a way that works best for you, your unique lifestyle, and what you know your body needs.

FOOD CHOICES I AVOID

Aside from the obvious things to avoid—processed, fried, and fast foods—there are other foods and situations I try to avoid whenever possible.

1. *Large portions:* At restaurants I often start with a full-sized salad with a vinaigrette and split an entrée or order a second protein-heavy appetizer like salmon tartar for my main course. This is a great way to sample new things on a menu and satisfy your appetite without overdoing it.

2. *Carb concentration:* I love pizza—it is one of my favorite exceptions to the principle of avoiding white flour. To compensate, I eat a slice or two of pizza and then balance it out with a lot of salad and a vegetable side, like broccoli or sautéed or steamed spinach. I also avoid the sugary fizzy drinks on the menu when I'm ordering pizza; instead of a Coke, I order a glass of red wine, an unsweetened iced tea, or water with lemon.

3. *Sugar:* Read the labels! Everyone knows that we need to avoid the high-fructose corn syrup and partially hydrogenated oils in processed foods, but white sugar is not much better for you. Sugar is everywhere if you start looking for it—in most breads, in crackers, in pasta sauce . . . in fact, most packaged foods, even ones you might not consider "sweet," are chockful of sugar. Our bodies don't need this added sugar, so I try to avoid it whenever possible. Some fancy organic labels use cane juice in place of sugar, but don't be fooled—it's sugar all the same.

4. *Salt:* Avoid salt when you can. Salt makes you bloated, and not just in your tummy: it swells and puffs your eyes and face and is terrible for your blood pressure and your heart. As with sugar, many packaged and processed foods are loaded with salt. Be sure to check labels, choose low-sodium options, tell the waiter to ask the chef to hold the salt when you order in a restaurant, and go easy on the salt when you cook. There are so many other spices and flavors to explore!

5. *Cream sauces—no exceptions!* I don't have a lot of don'ts on my list, but cream is one of them. Does it taste good? Sure. Do you need it? No. Cream is full of saturated fat, it's very high in calories, and it's not healthy for your heart or your waist. Can you enjoy a healthy, balanced, and satisfying diet without ever consuming another bite of cream? Absolutely! I don't particularly like cream sauces, so this one isn't too hard for me. But then again, it's almost impossible to eat more than about two bites of any food covered in cream without tipping the scale, and that's just not my style. I would rather have an entire plate of steamed or grilled fish and vegetables than one bite of pasta with cream sauce.

Principle 3: Substitute for Satisfaction!

All of us need to feel satisfied. The trick is staying open-minded enough to let yourself try unfamiliar foods and to not be afraid to make a change in the go-to snacks and foods you think you can't live without. As you begin to make some of the substitutions, give yourself enough time to try these new whole foods. Pay attention to how they make you feel fuller and more balanced. You will adjust your thinking accordingly.

One of the best ways to incorporate healthy eating habits is to take your current way of eating and begin making changes at the margin. I have found this to be a great way to avoid feeling like I have to eliminate my favorite foods, and an important part of staying satisfied. For example, I changed my diet a few years ago to include more whole grains in place of white flour. Some of my favorite changes include:

- **Brown rice** (instead of white)

- **Whole-grain pasta** (instead of white)

- **Olive oil** (instead of butter) (I use olive oil on everything from mashed potatoes to cooked veggies to toast. Almost any recipe that calls for butter can be modified to use olive oil, the taste is terrific, and it's great for your heart.)

- **Herbs and spices** (instead of salt—a little garlic goes a long way!)

- **Dark buckwheat honey** (instead of sugar)

- **Old-fashioned oats** mixed with walnuts and fruit (in place of granola and boxed cereals, which can be sugary and overly processed, even the organic brands)

- **Sweet potatoes** (instead of white)

- **High-quality dark chocolate** (in place of chocolate bars or baked goods made with butter and white flour) (Move away from milk chocolate gradually by starting with a 55 percent cacao mix and working your way higher as your palate adjusts and you begin to enjoy the new taste.)

- **Air-popped popcorn** with sea salt and olive oil (instead of crisps) (Prepare this quick, inexpensive, and high-fiber snack yourself if you can't find it in the grocery store.)

You will find a complete list of healthy, delicious foods from which to choose in the very next chapter. For now, begin by thinking of the foods that are high in saturated fats or sugar that you might want to swap out. By and large, the emphasis here is to avoid white flour and sugar and to cut back on processed foods. Everyone is different when it comes to the foods they find satisfying. I am going to give you guidelines that will help you discover foods and meals that make you feel happy and satisfied—without skimping on taste and the pleasure of eating.

Substitution will help you build healthy habits and patterns without feeling deprived. Don't underestimate the importance of the small things you can do to take better care of yourself! Every little bit adds up, making a big difference when it comes to your health. I am not asking you to stop drinking coffee or to never have another sandwich when you can use unsweetened soya (or other nondairy milks) or skimmed milk in your coffee with a little dark honey and make the switch to whole-grain bread to achieve your Ballet Beautiful goals while keeping yourself satisfied. You do not have to live on salads and puréed vegetables or juice fasts to reach your goals! I eat meat, cheese, whole-

BEWARE OF SWEET DRINKS!

Remember the importance of staying hydrated? Your body can confuse thirst with hunger, and the best way to hydrate is with water. I drink lots of water throughout the day and avoid sugary beverages and fizzy drinks, whether diet or regular. Sugary beverages are loaded with calories I would prefer to eat than drink, and I'm not a fan of sugar substitutes like aspartame and Splenda. And keep in mind that diet fizzy drinks are not good for you; they do have fewer calories because they are made with sugar substitutes, but they're unhealthy, and you will look and feel better without them. Dark fizzy drinks are particularly bad because they contain not only high-fructose corn syrup and caramel coloring but also phosphoric acid—an ingredient that will sap the strength of your bones and tax your kidneys. I have suffered from stress fractures before, and I can tell you that it isn't fun. As women, we all need to cautious about eating and drinking foods that are high in calcium to increase our bone density rather than deplete it! So cut out sugary beverages and keep your bones strong by drinking water or unsweetened iced tea with fresh lemon. When it comes to drinking dairy alternatives like soya, almond, or rice milk, I choose an unsweetened version. I also stick to organic skimmed milk, even in my coffee.

wheat pasta, and chocolate and drink wine regularly. But I also make an effort to choose skimmed milk for my coffee and cereal, I eat roasted potatoes instead of fried, and I squeeze in 15 or 30 minutes of exercise if I don't have time to do a full hour.

Principle 4: Be Flexible!

Flexibility is the key to building a balanced, satisfying lifestyle and the enemy of the negative mindset that can undermine your feeling of self-control when it comes to food. When I left the New York City Ballet, I didn't work out for a solid year. I had a lot of misconceptions about what foods were "good" and "bad" based on my experience with dieting in the past. As soon as I relaxed my "rules" about what I could and couldn't eat and became more flexible when it came to my relationship with food and my body, I started learning how to eat differently and become more flexible. I not only learned how to forgive myself for getting off track if I overdid it at a meal, but I soon lost 10 pounds—fast!

It was a real lesson for me. Becoming more flexible with my eating allowed me to feel satisfied and to stop obsessing over ice cream and chocolate-covered caramels. I found

Don't Be Afraid of Carbs!

There was a time when I was scared of eating carbs. Everyone said that carbs are fattening and talked about how great they looked when they didn't eat carbs, and that made me think I should avoid them too. This was the 2000s and low-carb diets were all the rage! I succumbed to this silly fad like many others. But in the process I also learned a lot about what works best for my body—most notably that, for me, avoiding carbs is a very bad idea. Eating the *right* carbs, I discovered, can help me whether I am trying to lose weight or maintain my weight (two very different goals—more on that later).

With no carbs in my diet, I was constantly hungry and grouchy. I had unbelievable cravings for sweets, and I think that leaving carbs out of my diet set me up for weight gain in the end. Today whole grains are a staple of my diet and the center of many of my favorite meals. Whole grains provide long-lasting energy and tons of fiber without spiking your blood sugar. I consider them key to keeping your waist slim, your heart healthy, and your appetite under control!

that when I made whole grains and healthy carbs a regular part of my life I suddenly craved less sugar, ate less sugar, and started losing weight.

There are many myths that can sabotage us if we let them. For example, eating at night will not make you fat. This myth has terrified so many women. Many of my clients have asked questions like: "How do I not eat after 6:00 PM? I work until then!" or, "Do I need to eat early, when I feed my kids? I like to wait for my partner to have dinner."

The truth is that it doesn't matter very much when you eat if you are eating often and eating good foods. If you go to bed at 8:00 PM, you may not want to eat past 6:00. But if you are awake later, eating later is fine. I'm not advocating a big meal at 11:00 PM with espresso and a rich dessert, but having dinner at nine o'clock is not going to ruin your figure. I eat a late dinner all the time—after all, I live in New York City! If I had a rule about not eating after 7:00 PM I would never have another dinner out with friends. In fact, I probably wouldn't eat dinner at all because I can't remember the last time I sat down to dinner before seven at night.

Do make an effort to go easy on your alcohol, sugar, and salt consumption, no matter what time of night you are eating. Too much of any of these could disrupt your sleep cycle, make you feel bloated, and lead you to overeat the next day.

Everyone is different in how and when they like to eat. You need to think about and figure out what works best for you. I personally prefer to eat four meals a day. I eat breakfast around 7:00 AM, then I split lunch in two—maybe half a sandwich and fruit around noon, then another small lunch around 4:00 or 5:00 PM. I eat dinner on the late side, usually around 9:00 PM. This might mean I have a small snack before my dinner, around 6:30 or 7:00 PM, but I rarely snack again before bed.

If you work in an office you might not have this flexibility, and if you're a busy mom you may prefer to eat with your kids. As you tune in to how your body is feeling—full, hungry and just right, then you will be able to decide how and when to eat so that you feel your best all day long.

Here's another myth that can get in the way of being flexible: you need to eat three square meals a day, no snacking allowed. When it comes to eating, our bodies need different amounts of food and at different times. *One size does not fit all.* It's true about fashion, and the same thing goes for what you eat. I'm not going to tell you to eat six mini-meals or three square meals a day with no snacks. Every body is different, and every day is different—for every one of us! I have clients who are grazers by nature and feel best when eating mini-meals all day long. But that doesn't work for everyone—the key is to find what works for you.

Many diets seem to chain you to your kitchen and your home to make you stay away from trouble. I find these types of eating plans very unrealistic because they are utterly inflexible. I will show you how to navigate restaurant eating and meals on the road, and I'll give you a usable guide to making the best possible choices when you don't have an ideal menu offering.

Katherine on Staying Away from Extremes

I now stay away from extremes. I learned that you can make simple substitutions that go a long way in how you look and feel—have a piece of cake and it doesn't have to mean your day is shot. I used to have a triple whole milk latte twice a day, every day; after Mary Helen and I talked about switching to soya or skimmed milk, I made the change and began to adjust. Now I don't miss it in a way that's important to me. I now indulge in a full-fat latte maybe once or twice a month. I also have to say that when I feel healthy and fit, I don't want to eat a whole cake. The times when I want to eat a whole cake are when I'm feeling lousy because I have already eaten a whole cake!

Keep in mind that this program will change the way you live, with flexibility built in. All you need to think about are your own needs and how to embrace them! Just don't forget to eat breakfast every day. Please!

Principle 5: Forgive Yourself and Move On!

Most of us have tried and failed when it comes to dieting. Because most diet programs provide temporary weight loss, we are often left with misconceived notions about dieting and how to lose weight. The problem with these programs is that they cannot be maintained, and so they set you up for failure and the dangerous swing of weight loss followed by weight gain.

All women struggle with forgiveness. To be truly happy and healthy, you must find a way to focus on the positive and do what you can do today to make tomorrow better.

Forget about the fact that you skipped your workout yesterday, ate fries earlier in the week, and had a brownie with lunch. Health is not all or nothing, and your approach to exercise and eating shouldn't be either!

This is true whether you've eaten dessert two nights in a row because it's holiday time or you're on vacation and have had cocktails at dusk for three straight days. My approach to getting in shape and staying in shape is all about forgiveness: if you miss two or three or even five days of working out, I will help you get right back into your schedule *when you can.* By being flexible and forgiving yourself, you can learn to move on when you have too much chocolate cake or polish off a bag of crisps without even thinking. Learning to forgive yourself and move forward with your healthy lifestyle even when you don't make great food choices or miss your workout allows you to regain your balance by making the next meal a healthy one. Treating your body with this type of kindness is truly liberating. It's a critical step on the road to a healthy relationship with your body and with food.

There was a time when my relationship with food was more guilty than forgiving. If I ate an extra slice of pizza or let myself enjoy a cookie, I felt like I'd "blown it" and might as well eat a chocolate bar and anything else I wanted or craved because I would make up for it by not eating enough calories the following day. Maybe you've been there too. But once I learned to be flexible and more forgiving, I found that balance became easy for me, that I could stop this destructive behavior and move on. As I learned to pay more attention to my body, I also realized that once or twice a month my hormones make me crave salty, oily foods like french fries, and that's okay. I can eat a salad for the next meal, drink some water or tea with lemon, and move on.

WHAT ABOUT FASTING?

My clients ask me all the time for my thoughts on fasting. The answer? I'm not a fan. I worked hard to achieve a balanced, healthy lifestyle and would be very wary of anything that might disrupt it. I also think that cleansing encourages bingeing because of its built-in deprivation. While I enjoy the occasional green juice, now that I know the beauty of balance in a healthy lifestyle, I'm just not interested. You do not need to fast with Ballet Beautiful; you only need to focus on filling your body with whole, nourishing, delicious foods and giving your body a challenging workout. Satisfaction, not deprivation, is the word here.

Chapter 8

The Ballet Beautiful
Kitchen

This chapter is chockful of easy-to-use lists of foods to help you substitute for satisfaction, reinforce your weight loss (if that is your desired goal), and live Ballet Beautifully. There are also tips here for shopping and stocking your refrigerator and cupboard with the foods that will always satisfy you—for breakfast, lunch, dinner, and snacks, and some desserts as well!

Whole Healthy Foods:
Lists to Live Ballet Beautifully

The food lists provided here essentially cover all the basic food groups—lean proteins, fibrous fruits and vegetables, grains, and dairy. I've even included sweet dessert options as well as healthy fats (including some dairy options, olive oil, and nuts). Most importantly, you'll find foods here that are easy to find at your local grocery or health food store and easy to incorporate into your life. I aim for a mix of lean protein, healthy fats, fiber, and grains at each meal. This balanced approach to food keeps me satisfied and well nourished.

As you get to know your timing and settle on some dishes or snacks to try, try using these lists to prepare your meals. As I've mentioned, I don't recommend fixating on or worrying about portion sizes—especially if you are eating unprocessed whole foods, with sweet treats in moderation.

Protein

These are suggestions and guidelines—feel free to discover your own favorites!

Fish and Seafood

I try to buy seafood that is fresh, local, and in season whenever possible!

Salmon (preferably wild)

Cod

Red snapper

Blue Fish

Flounder

Swordfish

Tuna steak

Prawns

Scallops

Mussels (a favorite bistro meal! Order mussels with a garlic and white wine sauce—*not* cream!)

Oysters (I eat them raw, not fried)

Red Meat and Poultry

Yes, meat can be a healthy part of your diet! Choose organic versions of the following when possible:

Extra-lean ground beef

Filet of beef

Skinless chicken breast (I eat the skin sometimes, as you'll see in some of the later recipes; again, everything in moderation!)

Top sirloin

Turkey breast

Lean ground turkey

Alternative Protein Sources (Including Beans and Nuts)

Beans (black, white, pinto, kidney, cannellini)

Eggs (free-range, organic)

Lentils

Butter beans

Nut butter (Almond and peanut butter are my favorites, though there are other varieties, such as cashew. Whatever you choose, read the labels and make sure you choose an organic option with no added sugar or oil.)

Nuts

Raw walnuts

Raw almonds

Raw cashews

Unsalted pistachios (undyed!)

Tofu

Soybeans or edamame

Dairy

Dairy can be a good source of calcium, protein, and vitamin D, but it can also contain too much fat. So be mindful of your cheese selections and try to stick with skimmed milk. (If you are vegetarian or vegan, you can get your calcium from your veggies, especially leafy greens.)

Fat-free plain Greek yogurt

Cottage cheese

Organic string cheese (great for snacks and when you are on the go)

Feta cheese

Organic skimmed milk

Fresh, low-salt mozzarella cheese

Extra-sharp Cheddar cheese

There are plenty of nondairy substitutes out there. Almond milk is my personal favorite, but soya and rice milk can also be great ways to go. Just check the labels—look for an unsweetened variety, as some nondairy products have added sugars.

Grains

I love the sustained energy that whole grains give me, especially on days when I am working out.

Whole-wheat or multi-grain bread

Whole-wheat tortillas or wraps for sandwiches

Whole-wheat pasta

Quinoa pasta or brown rice pasta

Wild rice

Quinoa

Whole-grain cereals, including steel-cut oats, Shredded Wheat, and old-fashioned oats

Weetabix (whole-grain cereal)

Oat bran

Whole-grain crackers and rice cakes (These are packaged foods and, as such, not exactly "clean eating." But they also are good sources of fiber.)

Vegetables

I use vegetables that are versatile and can be prepared in a variety of ways. Frozen spinach, for instance, can be a good choice in the winter, when good fresh veggies are hard to find. Carrots, peppers, and kale are among the vegetables that work well cooked or raw.

Spinach

Broccoli

Kale

Spring greens (leafy greens are terrific sources of calcium—great for your bones as well as your waist!)

Squash

Fresh green beans

Asparagus

Carrots

Brussels sprouts

Aubergine

Yams or sweet potatoes

Onions

Peppers (green, red, yellow, or orange)

Celery

Courgette

Tomatoes

Lettuce (Buy organic when possible, and buy all types: cos, rocket, mixed greens—whatever you like best! But avoid iceberg: it doesn't have the nutritional impact of other greens.)

Mushrooms

Cucumbers

Fruits

When choosing fruit, remember that it's always best to eat what is in season!

Blueberries

Raspberries

Strawberries

Grapefruit

Apples

Oranges

Bananas (in moderation because bananas are relatively high in sugar—and the riper they are, the higher the sugar content)

Avocados

Kiwis

Pears

Peaches and nectarines

Plums

Cherries

Melons

Tropical fruits (fresh mangoes, papaya, pineapple)

Watermelon

Spices

Spices are a great way to add flavor and avoid salt. The following are some of my favorites—but use what you like! I find the taste for herbs and spices to be pretty individual. Experiment, but don't force yourself to eat something you don't like. And remember, these are guidelines—you don't have to walk through the grocery store with this list in hand! Fresh spices have a slightly different taste and flavor in foods and dishes, but they are not always available. Fortunately, the many high-quality dried spices available can bring a dish alive!

Coriander

Garlic

Ginger

Cayenne pepper

Red chili flakes

Rosemary

Dill

Lemon pepper

Parsley

Cumin

Fresh basil

Condiments and Dressings

With a base of olive oil, vinegar, and a little Dijon mustard, you can make most any sauce or vinaigrette!

Extra-virgin olive oil

Rapeseed oil

Balsamic vinegar

Red and white wine vinegar

Fresh lemon (delicious squeezed over a steak or grilled chicken)

Dijon mustard

Cream-free, vegetable- or bean-based spreads like tapenade, hummus, and baba ghanoush

Dark honey (buckwheat is my favorite)

Maple syrup

Fat-free plain yogurt as a base for healthy herb-flavored sauces and dips

Dill sauce made with plain fat-free yogurt

Spice Up Your Meals in a Healthy Way!

Many prepackaged salad dressings, dips, and marinades are full of saturated fats, sugar, and a long list of other ingredients that I cannot even begin to pronounce. Avoid them by making your own! Adding spices to plain yogurt is a great, simple way to make a dip or sauce. And a simple French vinaigrette can go a long way to add flavor to fish and meat without a lot of calories. Here are two of my favorites that take no time to prepare.

Quick and Easy Yogurt Dip

Great as an alternative to hummus for dipping fresh veggies or as a substitute for mayo on your favorite sandwich!
Combine a pot of nonfat or low-fat Greek yogurt with the juice from half a fresh lemon, a small chopped cucumber, a small clove of garlic, chopped, and fresh herbs of your choice.

French Vinaigrette

Not only good on a green salad but a delicious marinade for fish!
Mix equal parts extra-virgin olive oil, maple syrup, and Dijon mustard. Add a sprinkle of fresh pepper and one chopped clove of garlic, and whisk together.

Drinks

Spa water (Making your own doesn't take much time, and it really feels like a treat! Combine filtered water with ice and fresh lemon or cucumber slices in a beautiful glass pitcher.)

Sparkling water

Organic coffee or tea (I drink tea with caffeine and also herbal teas, but avoid decaffeinated teas because of my concerns about the process of removing caffeine.)

Red wine (in moderation)

Prepared and Packaged Foods

While "clean eating" means passing up prepared and packaged foods, I believe in everything in moderation. Listed here are the foods I keep on hand that are healthy and quick to prepare. Keeping your home stocked with these foods makes it easy to say no to fast food and delivery. Notice that the list includes frozen fruits and veggies; if you can't find them in season, frozen can be a great substitute—just be sure to check package labels to make sure you're buying pure produce and avoid those with added sweeteners or salt. Speaking of salt, some of the items on this list are fairly salty, so enjoy in moderation.

- Canned albacore tuna in water or olive oil
- Low-sodium, organic canned soups
- Canned or jarred Greek or Italian olives
- Jarred artichoke hearts
- Jarred roasted peppers
- Cornichons (as appetizers before dinner)
- Whole-grain, trans-fat-free crispbreads
- Brown rice cakes
- Frozen vegetables (green peas, spinach, broccoli, carrots)
- Frozen fruit (berry mixes for smoothies)
- Premade pasta sauces that don't use sugar (read the labels) or too much salt
- Fresh whole-grain pasta and ravioli (buy extras and keep them in the freezer)
- Organic, low-sodium deli meats
- Organic Porridge
- Half Naked Olive Oil Popcorn
- Green & Black Organic Dark Chocolate (60 percent cacao or higher)

Cooking and Meal Preparation Tips

As you can see, my food list covers a lot of food! I try to stick to fresh, whole, nutrient-rich foods that, incidentally, don't require as much fussing when it comes time to cook. It's unrealistic to make everything from scratch, and Ballet Beautiful is about attaining a healthy and realistic lifestyle! So when I do choose and eat packaged foods, I carefully read the labels to make sure that, like the whole foods in my diet, they're high in fiber and nutrients while low in salt, sugar, and unhealthy fats.

Most of the foods on my list are easy to prepare. In general, with meats, fish, and poultry, I do a lot of grilling and quick sautéing. I use my mom's rule of thumb for using the oven: avoid it in the summer months, when the kitchen is already warm, and roast and bake more frequently in the cold winter months when you are happy to heat up the house. When it comes to cooking time, you can't beat the speed of steaming vegetables—or the health benefits! Sautéing is fast too, but go easy on the oil, especially if you're preparing vegetables that tend to be very absorbent, like broccoli or mushrooms. If the grill is already hot, I almost always throw a veggie side on to save time.

I try to balance my days eating out and eating in, and I don't eat whole-wheat pasta for dinner, for instance, on days when I have a sandwich or bagel for lunch. I'll opt for a salad or greens with lean protein, and vice versa. If I don't have time to cook brown rice, I'll make quinoa or steam or roast sweet potatoes. In other words, I use the principle of flexibility in preparing meals to help me reach my goals each day.

Shopping Tips

When buying groceries, I always start with the fresh foods, fill up my cart, and go from there.

1. *First stop—produce!* Stocking up on lots of fruits and vegetables is the perfect starting point for my healthy shopping cart. To make my life easier during the workweek, I include items like precut celery and baby carrots (a favorite afternoon or predinner snack with hummus), peeled garlic, and organic prepacked salads. I also love apples, pears, clementines, plums, and basically any fruit that I can throw in my bag or car in the morning and eat during the day when I am out. I know it sounds silly, but I'm a lot more likely to eat fresh citrus if I have easy-to-peel clementines on hand instead of navel oranges, so that's what I buy! Think easy, fast, and fresh.

2. *Second stop—whole grains!* I love the sustained energy that whole grains give me! Carbs are good, remember? I find that they satisfy me even more when I mix them with a bit of protein and healthy fats—such as adding walnuts to breakfast porridge, having some cheese, olives, or natural peanut butter with whole-grain crispbreads, or eating avocado slices on whole-grain toast.

3. *Next up—high-quality, lean proteins!* My favorites are organic chicken, eggs (I keep hard-boiled eggs in the fridge to toss in salads or eat while I'm prepping a meal if I'm starving!), lean cuts of red meat, wild salmon, lentil soup, beans, and snack or breakfast foods like non- or low-fat Greek yogurt.

4. *Don't forget healthy fats!* I find that eating some variety of olive oil, nuts, and avocados every day is a key to feeling satisfied.

5. *Top up your cart with a few high-quality treats!* Dark chocolate is one of my favorite daily indulgences. (You know by now that my current favorite is Green & Black's Dark, either 70 or 85 percent cacao mix.) I also really love cheese—mozzarella, sharp Cheddar, and blue cheese are all favorites. Living Ballet Beautifully doesn't mean giving up Brie (I adore triple cream cheese!), but indulge in moderation. You can have treats while living the Ballet Beautiful lifestyle—absolutely! Again, moderation and flexibility are key.

MY FAVORITE SNACKS AND MEALS

Breakfast: The Must-Eat Meal!

- I try to start my day with a green tea with fresh lemon, though I often have coffee with skimmed milk instead.
- My go-to breakfast is old-fashioned porridge with walnuts and a little bit of dried fruit mixed in. I add dried, naturally sweetened cherries and prunes to my shopping cart.

Lunch

- Fresh salad leaves with mozzarella and tomatoes or grilled salmon, with whole-grain crackers or a whole-wheat pita and hummus on the side. I generally dress my salads with olive oil and vinegar or a bit of fresh lemon juice.
- I like to finish off lunch with fresh fruit and a hot tea or coffee.

Snacks

Depending on how hungry I am, I choose one of the following afternoon snacks:

- A piece of fruit with some raw almonds or cashew nuts
- A cereal bowl of fresh popcorn with olive oil and a little salt with an orange or fruit in season.
- A few whole-grain crispbreads with cottage cheese
- Sprouted cinnamon toast with peanut butter (works for breakfast or lunch too, with fresh fruit!)
- Dried fruit, especially naturally sweetened cherries and prunes

Dinner

- I like to include a fresh salad and lots of veggies, whenever possible, especially in the summer months.
- My favorite is organic roast chicken with salad and a quick veggie side like sautéed or steamed spinach. On weeknights I grab a prepared chicken from a store like Whole Foods. If I have time on the weekend, I might roast a chicken or pork tenderloin from scratch, with sweet potatoes, onions, garlic, and celery.
- If I want a vegetarian option, I try to think about protein, especially if I worked out in the afternoon. Beans and quinoa are great ways to get protein. My brother John's vegetarian chili with a big salad and sautéed greens on the side is a favorite choice. (See his recipe on page 230).

Eating Out

Eating out can really be challenging because the food is often full of fat and salt and temptation abounds! But the principles of flexibility and preparation will help keep you connected to your Ballet Beautiful lifestyle, no matter where you choose to eat. Learning how to make dining out a healthy experience is a skill, but one that is easy to learn and apply.

Before the meal, avoid sugary cocktails. Order a glass of wine or just drink sparkling water. Drinking a sugary drink (with fruit juice or a fizzy drink) before dinner sets you up to overeat. If you want a cocktail, have some soda water with a splash of vodka and a slice of lime.

1. *Start with a salad:* Always start with a salad, avoiding the salad dressing dump that many restaurants unfortunately do by ordering yours with olive oil and vinegar on the side. I sometimes use this technique when I order a wedge salad at a steakhouse: get some blue cheese on the side instead of blue cheese dressing and order the salad with olive oil and vinegar. I get to enjoy the freshness of the greens and tomatoes and the tanginess of the blue cheese (which I love!) without the guilt of consuming a heavy, creamy dressing. I can then build the salad my way and enjoy every bite!

2. *Hold the salt:* This little tip has changed my relationship with restaurant food. Many chefs douse their food in salt and unnecessary sodium. When you're ordering out, ask the waiter to ask the chef to hold the salt—and the butter. It's shocking how much most restaurants use of both.

3. *Skip the sauce:* If there is a sauce in your order, ask for it on the side unless it is your pasta. If it is a cream sauce, tell them not to even bring it, or swap it for a marinara.

4. *When in doubt, order grilled:* Grilled options are almost always a lighter, guilt-free way to enjoy your favorite meats and fish.

5. *Skip the bread and crisps:* You can live without it. If you are going to eat bread with your meal, request whole-grain and use olive oil rather than butter. Don't eat it dry! The oil will help satisfy and tame your appetite.

6. *Order water with your meal:* Stay hydrated to regulate your hunger.

7. *Watch your portions:* Try an appetizer with a salad as a meal, or split an entrée to save money and calories!

8. *Hold off on dessert:* Have a herbal tea or decaf coffee and a side of berries or sorbet if you have to have desert. I usually just wait until I get home to eat my favorite dark chocolate.

9. *Use substitutions:* Remember—it's about substitution, not deprivation. Often you can find something delicious that's also a healthier option if you ask the waiter. I often order sautéed greens with my eggs at brunch instead of bacon. Use your substitution principle!

Traveling and Eating:
Two Fussy Companions

It can be overwhelming to make good food choices when eating out or traveling makes so many options available. I always find that sticking to a version of what works for me at home keeps me looking and feeling my best when I am on the go. Traveling and flying especially can be incredibly dehydrating. I always make an effort to drink extra water on travel days to make up for the loss of fluids, and I make sure I'm eating because I'm hungry, not because I'm tired and thirsty.

Breakfast can be one of the most confusing meals when you travel because of the vast and overwhelming array of choices on hotel buffets and menus. Unless it's a special occasion, I don't alter my meals dramatically just because I am on the road. This helps keep my weight steady and prevents crashes from spikes in blood sugar. The concept here also applies to working out: you don't have to ditch your workout because you are in a hotel. Just modify it and work with your surroundings. I will often choose a plain low-fat yogurt sprinkled with raw almonds (brought from home!) as a source of protein and fat, with some fresh fruit and a slice of whole-grain toast. Be wary of flavored yogurts—most are full of sugar, sometimes even glucose syrup. Fresh-cut fruit or hard-boiled eggs are good options. And coffee or tea, of course!

I usually bypass the standard breakfast meat (salty) and juice (extra sugar) and opt for hardy grains, yogurt, and fresh local fruit instead. When I'm traveling, this healthy and delicious fruit-filled breakfast helps me power through my morning Ballet Beautiful exercises and leaves me feeling great until lunch. For lunch and dinner, I look for fresh salads and lots of vegetables, with lean proteins like chicken or fish. I also ask for sauce or dressing on the side so that I can control the portion.

One of the difficulties in traveling is the unknown, but small tricks like these can make all the difference in keeping your weight consistent. Healthy Ballet Beautiful-style meals will do wonders for your energy level and your waist by keeping you energized and satisfied and your metabolism humming, even when you are on the go.

Chapter 9

Putting It All Together

What a Ballet Beautiful Week Looks Like

We have talked a lot about finding balance and satisfaction in your diet. For me, mixing whole grains with healthy fats, protein, and fresh fruit and vegetables at every snack or meal is the key. This chapter is going to show you how to bring your Ballet Beautiful kitchen to life through delicious, wholesome meals in a format that may help you think about how to eat more frequently, make sensible substitutions, and stay on track with how you feel.

Below you'll find Seven Days of Snacks and Meals—all flexible and easy to prepare. I'm also including sample workouts for an ideal, moderate, and light week so that you can start to envision how to incorporate your new Ballet Beautiful lifestyle and workout into your everyday life!

Although I tend to eat the same breakfast, I have offered some other healthy options that will leave you feeling energetic and satisfied. And remember, don't skip breakfast! When I'm on the run, it's hard for me to find time to prepare lunch—

though, as I mentioned in the previous chapter, I do tend to eat two little lunches spaced out through the afternoon. Consider these options and then add in your own alternatives.

I have the most fun and variety with dinner. I do eat out often, but I've included my Flash Cooking Tips to help you prepare meals that are simple, quick, and delicious—whether you are cooking just for yourself or for friends and family too!

→ Seven Breakfasts

1. Old-fashioned porridge with walnuts and fresh blueberries. This is my go-to on days when I am training. If you can't manage old-fashioned oats because you're traveling or you're very short on time, try instant oats with no added sugars or preservatives. Note too that even Starbucks sells porridge these days, which makes it easier to eat well on the road!

2. Two hard-boiled eggs with one slice of whole-grain toast drizzled with olive oil and half a grapefruit or an orange. You can boil the eggs the night before to save on time!

3. Plain, fat-free Greek yogurt with walnuts and five dried pitted prunes.

4. A whole-grain English muffin with cottage cheese and fresh berries. If you are running out the door, wrap it in aluminum foil—the heat of the toasted muffins will melt the cheese. Yum!

5. Weetabix cereal with raw almonds and raspberries. I sometimes add old-fashioned porridge to the mix.

6. One slice of toasted whole-grain bread or a whole-grain bagel with half an avocado drizzled with olive oil, sea salt, and red pepper flakes.

7. Two brown rice cakes or crispbreads with fresh peanut or almond butter and an apple or pear. I'm not necessarily advocating crispbreads for breakfast, but when you are rushing this really does the trick!

➥ Seven Midmorning Snacks

I don't find that I need a snack midmorning every day—it's all about how early I get up. Here are some of my lighter go-tos when hunger strikes!

1. A piece of fruit and tea

2. A handful of raw, unsalted nuts

3. Whole-grain crackers or raw veggies with hummus

4. An avocado with olive oil and sea salt over quinoa

5. Half a small bran muffin with tea

6. Three brown rice cakes with a glass of almond or skimmed milk

7. Half a whole-wheat pita with low-fat goat's cheese and honey

➥ Seven Lunches

I love a vegetarian soup or a big salad for lunch! In the summer months I might swap the chili for a gazpacho.

1. A large green salad with grilled chicken, tomatoes, fresh mushrooms, and red peppers, and whole-grain crackers (This is great after a morning workout when your body needs the extra protein.)

2. Spinach salad with grilled salmon, cucumber, tomatoes, and red onions, and a small whole-grain roll

3. Lentil soup with an apple or pear and cottage cheese

4. Vegetarian chili with a side of steamed greens

5. Toasted whole-grain bread or half a whole-wheat bagel with natural peanut butter and a piece of fruit

6. Two-egg omelet with onion and tomatoes, a green salad, and whole-grain toast

7. Aubergine ratatouille over quinoa

➔ Seven Afternoon Snacks

1. An organic apple with a handful of raw almonds and a brown rice cake

2. Celery and carrot slices or wheat crackers with hummus

3. Five to 10 olives with cherry tomatoes

4. Air-popped popcorn with sea salt and olive oil, and fresh fruit

5. A hard-boiled egg and grape tomatoes

6. Dry, roasted, unsalted peanuts and five pitted prunes

7. Leftover cooked veggies from last night's dinner

➔ Seven Dinners

I mix things up a bit by making sure I don't eat an entrée salad for lunch and dinner or soup twice in one day!

1. An entrée-size salad with cos lettuce, tomatoes, avocado, and canned tuna in olive oil

2. Roast chicken with a fresh green salad with mushrooms and avocado and steamed broccoli

3. Baked or Grilled salmon with steamed or sautéed greens, sweet potatoes, and a side salad

4. Roasted vegetables with baked flounder in olive oil lemon sauce and a fresh tomato-avocado salad

5. Whole-grain pasta with fresh tomato and spinach, with a large green salad on the side

6. Grilled lean steak with grilled onion, squash, and courgette slices and steamed asparagus

7. Vegetable soup with steamed broccoli and quinoa avocado salad

➜ Seven Desserts

1. Two to three ounces of a high-quality dark chocolate bar

2. A bowl of fresh berries or fruit, topped with yogurt

3. An almond milk and fresh berry smoothie

4. Baked cinnamon apples with walnuts

5. A few bites of a favorite cheese with red wine

6. Two to three digestive biscuits with skimmed or almond milk

7. A few Gingernut biscuits with hot herbal tea

Sample Workouts—A Guide to Building Your New Ballet Beautiful Body!

The sample meals above are the perfect accompaniment to your Ballet Beautiful program, no matter what your fitness level at this time. Now I'll give you a few ideas on how to put your work from Part II together with your healthy new lifestyle to maximize your Ballet Beautiful body!

These combinations are organized into three categories: an ideal week (workouts on five to six days), a moderate week (three to four workouts), and a light week (one to three workouts). We all are busy, so from week to week many of us shift from ideal to moderate to light, then back again. Remember that even on days when you cannot work out you can stick with your Ballet Beautiful lifestyle by simply eating healthy and sticking to the food lists in Chapter 8. Use your Ballet Beautiful principles to guide and ground you. Then, when you have more time to work out, you can maximize your results!

An Ideal Week

We don't live in an ideal world, but you can work to make time in your life for an ideal week with Ballet Beautiful! The results from these workouts, done two to three weeks in a row, will be more than worth every minute of your time.

Five to six days: 60-Minute Classic Ballet Beautiful Workout: This is my personal workout, and I love the way it has changed my body and kept me strong but graceful!

Or:
Three days: Classic Ballet Beautiful Workout

Two to three days: Full Blast Series Workout

A Moderate Week

Three days: 60-Minute Classic Ballet Beautiful Workout

Or:

Two days: 60-Minute Classic Ballet Beautiful Workout

One day: Full Ballet Beautiful Blast Series Workout

A Light Week

Five days: 15- to 30-Minute Ballet Beautiful Workout: Even if you barely have time for working out, I recommend doing a little every day to stay connected to your Ballet Beautiful body and help you keep your focus too. Doing a short, 15-Minute Blast four to five days a week is a great way to approach the program when you are really tight on time. Or if you can only squeeze in two days of workouts, try for two 15-Minute Blasts; even this will remind your body how to keep its tone and strength. And if you can manage to work out 30 minutes a day, even better!

AMY ON BALLET BEAUTIFUL

Amy says, "I have a little one, and I am exhausted all the time, so it's hard for me to find an hour to work out. With Ballet Beautiful, I can make time for 15 minutes. The Blasts energize me, and I often will do a second Blast and stretch it to 30 minutes on days when I didn't think I had it in me! One Blast or a portion of the Classic Workout five days a week is a commitment that I can keep, and it inspires a lot of confidence in myself!"

Here's a sample schedule from one of Amy's weeks:

Monday: Ballet Beautiful Full-Body Blast, with Swan Arms if there's extra time

Tuesday: Ballet Beautiful Plié Series, with a Full-Body Blast when there's time

Wednesday: Ballet Beautiful Bridge Series and the Reverse Bridge from the Classic Workout

Thursday: Abs Workout from the Classic and the Arabesque Series from the Blast

Friday: Inner and Outer Thigh Series from the Classic and Swan Arms

Now that we have the workouts down, let's talk about how to make it happen in your Ballet Beautiful kitchen!

Ballet Beautiful Recipes

When I prepare food for myself, I always try to keep it as simple, fresh, and fast as possible! I am not a chef and have no professional training in the kitchen. I do love great food and enjoy rewarding my body with fresh, healthy meals—especially after a hard workout! I have two different strategies for cooking that help me balance my busy schedule with fun, nutritious, stress-free meals:

1. *"Flash cooking" for weeknights:* Flash-cooked meals are quick and easy to prepare using a combination of healthy prepared foods and fresh local fruits and veggies.

2. *Health-conscious homemade meals:* When I have more time, I make fresh, delicious, health-conscious meals from scratch.

Flash-Cooking Recipes

I am an expert at flash-cooking, and I encourage all of my clients to learn this easy cooking strategy! Flash-cooking lets me save calories and money by eating at home without spending hours in the kitchen. I work within my eating principles and use healthy prepared foods, like an organic roast chicken or fresh whole-wheat ravioli, and combine them with fresh vegetables that I can prepare quickly, like a green salad or steamed spinach. Here are some of my favorite go-to flash recipes for dinner and lunch.

⇢ Slice and Serve a Precooked Organic Roast Chicken with Green Salad

You can make green salad with whatever is in the kitchen: tomatoes, baby carrots, celery, and sunflower seeds for crunch. A side of fresh apple or pear slices and sharp Cheddar cheese completes this speedy, healthy meal.

→ Green Salad

SERVES TWO TO FOUR

Enough lettuce greens to serve
two to four people
100g (3 ½oz) chopped tomatoes or a
handful of grape tomatoes, washed
2 stalks of celery, diced
6 baby carrots, diced
1 tablespoon roasted sunflower seeds,
no salt
Olive oil
Sea salt
Freshly ground pepper
1 fresh lemon
2 apples, sliced, or 2 pears, sliced
Sharp Cheddar cheese, for garnish

1. Mix the salad ingredients in a large bowl. Toss with olive oil, salt, and pepper. Squeeze the juice of the lemon over the salad. Toss again and serve.

2. Serve with sliced roast chicken, apple or pear slices, and sharp Cheddar cheese.

Note: If I choose to eat the skin on the chicken, I won't eat the cheese, and vice versa.

Serve Whole-Wheat Ravioli with Sautéed Spinach

SERVES FOUR

1 package of whole-wheat ravioli
1 jar of fresh tomato sauce from your local grocer or market (Remember to read the label and avoid a product with added sugar and high sodium!)
Parmesan cheese, for garnish
1 head of garlic (*Note:* If you are really pressed for time, buy pre-peeled garlic. It doesn't taste as good, but it does the trick and saves a ton of time!!)
Olive oil
2 packages of organic frozen spinach or 1 package of organic baby spinach
Freshly ground black pepper

1. Boil and drain the pasta. Cover with the jarred sauce. Top with parmesan cheese and serve.

2. Sauté the head of garlic in olive oil over medium heat until golden brown. Add the spinach and cook until warm and tender. Add freshly ground pepper.

→ Make Salad Your Entrée!

Quick, healthy, and delicious—an entrée salad is the perfect flash meal! You get all of your veggies, vitamins, and antioxidants plus lean protein in one bowl. An entrée salad is one of my favs when I am short on time. It's great for your figure too! If you keep your fridge stocked from the Ballet Beautiful shopping list, you'll always have ingredients on hand for quick and easy entrée salads. These recipes will get you started; if you want to get creative, you can always start with a base of greens and add veggies, lean protein like chicken or fish, and a simple dressing of vinegar and oil (three parts oil to one part vinegar).

➡ Salad with Tuna and Avocado

I love the combination of salty and sweet in this salad! It makes a great entrée on a weeknight or a terrific lunch on a summer day. The mix of protein, fiber, and healthy fats helps my body recover from a hard workout. Plus, it's easy to find the ingredients at any market and to store them at home!

1 package of organic mixed greens or
   spinach
1 can Italian tuna in olive oil
1 ripe avocado
2 small cucumbers, diced
40g (1 ½oz) dried fruit, diced (whatever
   you have—dried cherries, raisins, even
   sliced dried pears!)
12 raw almonds, diced
Freshly ground pepper
Balsamic vinegar
Olive oil

1. Place the salad leaves in a large bowl. Top with the tuna, including the oil from the can.

2. Slice the ripe avocado on top and sprinkle with the diced cucumbers, dried fruit, and almonds.

3. Grind fresh pepper over the salad and splash with Balsamic vinegar. Toss and serve with freshly toasted whole-grain bread drizzled with olive oil.

➻ Scrambled Eggs with Peppers and Onions and Salad

SERVES TWO TO THREE

I love this meal when I am eating late. It's satisfying, quick, and easy and doesn't keep me awake at night! When it comes to sautéing veggies with eggs, you can get creative. I've used peppers and onions (as with this recipe), but almost any vegetables in your fridge can make for a tasty addition to eggs, including tomatoes, mushrooms, courgette, or even fresh basil leaves.

½ sweet onion

Olive oil (Remember our substitution principle of olive oil in place of butter? Here you see it in action.)

2 Italian peppers

6 organic eggs (I always eat the full egg with yolk—egg whites do not do it for me!)

Freshly ground pepper

Handful of salad leaves

1 small fresh tomato, chopped

1 tablespoon Balsamic vinegar

1. Chop the onion and sauté in olive oil over medium-high heat. Wash, de-seed, and slice the Italian peppers (preferably organic or from your local market). Mix in the eggs and cook over medium heat. Add pepper to taste.

2. In a separate bowl, prepare the salad leaves and top with the chopped tomato (again, preferably local). In the winter you can use pear slices or even citrus, like orange slices. Coat with olive oil, Balsamic vinegar, and pepper. Toss.

Flash-Cook Your Lunch!

Here are some of my favorite recipes for fast, healthy lunches that will really satisfy you! Note that leftovers from the previous night's healthy meal can go a long way the next day and save a lot of time.

➥ Fresh Mozzarella Salad with Tomatoes and Hard-Boiled Eggs

SERVES TWO TO THREE

I love this salad on the weekends! It's filling, fresh, and tasty—a perfect light lunch!

1 head fresh, organic round lettuce

4 fresh basil leaves

1 large, vine-ripened, organic tomato

1 small shallot

2 hard-boiled eggs

100g (4oz) fresh mozzarella

1 tablespoon olive oil

1 tablespoon Balsamic vinegar

Freshly ground sea salt and pepper

2 whole-grain English muffins

1. Wash and tear the lettuce and basil leaves and place them in a large salad bowl.

2. Chop the tomato, shallot, hard-boiled eggs, and mozzarella and add them to the bowl. Coat with the olive oil and Balsamic vinegar and sprinkle on a little sea salt and pepper. Toss.

3. Serve with toasted English muffin halves topped with olive oil and a dash of sea salt.

➥ Spinach and Tomato with Quinoa

SERVES TWO TO THREE

This is another favorite lunch recipe that lets me build off leftovers. If you don't have cooked spinach in the fridge, you can quickly steam or sauté some spinach or even some kale with a few cherry tomatoes for the same effect!

350g (12oz) quinoa (make sure to rinse it well before using)

1 avocado

1 tablespoon olive oil

1 lemon

Sea salt

Leftover cooked spinach and tomato

1. Bring 1 litre (32fl oz) of water to a boil and add the quinoa. Cover. Lower the heat and simmer until the water is absorbed, about 15 to 20 minutes. In the meantime, chop the avocado.

2. Add the olive oil to the quinoa with the chopped avocado, the juice of half a lemon, and sea salt. Serve in soup bowls and top with leftover spinach and tomato or other veggies.

→ Hard-Boiled Eggs with Wheat Toast and Fruit

This meal is quick and easy and also very light. It's great for breakfast on the weekends, and I love it for lunch too. It will energize you without making you feel stuffed! You can also use leftover veggies or cottage cheese here in place of the eggs.

2 hard-boiled organic eggs
Freshly ground sea salt and pepper
Whole-grain toast, 1 slice
Olive oil
Fresh fruit, in season (an apple, a pear, a small bowl of berries)

1. Hard-boil and peel the eggs.

2. Mash with a fork on a plate and mix with salt and pepper.

3. Toast the bread and drizzle with olive oil. Serve with fresh fruit and a mug of hot tea with lemon.

Health-Conscious Homemade Meals

Here are a few of my favorite dishes that I make on days when I have more time. Enjoy!

→ Chicken with Mustard and Garlic and Steamed Asparagus with a Cucumber Tomato Salad

SERVES TWO

The mustard and garlic in this chicken recipe add tons of flavor without a lot of extra calories. With some veggies and salad, this is my favorite kind of meal! In the winter I would swap out the asparagus for roasted Brussels sprouts or cauliflower and baby carrots and throw it all in the oven together.

2 organic chicken breasts with skin
Olive oil
Freshly ground pepper
2 tablespoons Dijon mustard
4 cloves garlic
Fresh asparagus
2 small cucumbers
1 large, organic, vine-ripened tomato
3 medium-sized carrots, washed and
    peeled
Balsamic vinegar

1. Heat the oven to 200°C (400°F/Gas Mark 6). Wash and place the chicken in an oven-safe baking dish, skin side up. Drizzle with olive oil and freshly ground pepper, then coat each chicken breast liberally with mustard. Mince the garlic and sprinkle over the chicken. Bake for 30 minutes.

2. Steam the asparagus in a pot of boiling water for two minutes. Remove from the pot and rinse with cold water.

3. Chop the cucumbers, tomato, and carrots. Place in a bowl and drizzle with olive oil and Balsamic vinegar. Add freshly ground pepper and toss.

⇢ Roasted Salmon with Tomatoes and Olives, Sweet Potatoes, and Steamed Spinach

I love salmon! It's great for your skin, and for your waistline too. When I eat out, I always look for salmon on the menu, and it's a favorite to prepare at home.

2 medium-sized sweet potatoes

1 medium-sized sweet onion

Olive oil

Sea salt

Freshly ground pepper

680g (1 ½lb) wild salmon, organic, cut into 2 or 3 pieces

45g (1 ½oz) your favorite high-quality olives
    (I look for low-sodium pitted versions)

100g (3 ½oz) grape tomatoes or one whole tomato, chopped

1 package of organic spinach

1. Heat the oven to 200°C (400°F/Gas Mark 6). Cube the sweet potato and chop the onion. Combine in a roasting pan and drizzle with olive oil, sea salt, and fresh pepper. Bake for 45 to 50 minutes.

2. Rinse the salmon and place it in a baking dish with the olives and grape tomatoes (or chopped whole tomatoes). Drizzle with olive oil, on both sides of the fish, and finish with freshly ground pepper. Bake 20 minutes at 200°C (400°F/Gas Mark 6).

3. Meanwhile, steam a handful of spinach until it is soft and still a rich green color. (As it overcooks, spinach turns darker.) (*Note:* Kale makes a great substitute for spinach here.)

⇀ Vegetable Soup

SERVES FOUR

This vegetable soup is one of my favorites, especially in the winter months. Serve with whole-grain crackers, fresh fruit, and sharp Cheddar cheese.

1 large sweet onion

3 stalks celery

½ small cabbage

400g (14oz) cherry tomatoes

180g (6 ½oz) fresh tomatoes, diced

150g (5 ¼oz) butter beans

145g (5oz) green peas

100g (3 ½oz) okra

110g (4oz) green beans, sliced

1 large baking potato, diced

4 tablespoons fresh parsley, chopped

4 tablespoons light soy sauce

Pinch fresh ground pepper

Pinch sea salt

1. Bring two quarts of filtered water to a boil.

2. Finely chop or blend the onion, celery, and cabbage to create a thick base for your soup and add to the boiling water.

3. Add the cherry tomatoes and tomatoes, finely chopped but not peeled. Mix well and cook on medium heat.

4. Add all remaining ingredients. Simmer slowly and add filtered water as needed, stirring often for two to three hours.

→ Gazpacho

Gazpacho is a favorite during the summer months. It's not enough for a full meal, but it makes a great starter to a light, healthy meal of grilled fish and vegetables!

½ large sweet onion
90g (3 ¼oz) fresh tomatoes, peeled
   and seeded
75g (2 ¾oz) green pepper
50g (1 ¾oz) cucumber
50g (1 ¾oz) celery
½ clove garlic
475ml (16fl oz) tomato juice
1 teaspoon Worcestershire sauce
3 tablespoons rice wine vinegar
3 tablespoons olive oil
Fresh pepper
Sea salt

1. Finely chop all of the vegetables. Mince and add the garlic.

2. Add the tomato juice to the vegetables, along with the Worcestershire sauce, rice wine vinegar, and olive oil. Season to taste with freshly ground pepper and sea salt.

3. Mix well and refrigerate 24 hours or overnight in a glass container. Enjoy served cold in chilled bowls.

→ Pasta with Spinach and Tomato

SERVES FOUR

Spinach is a staple of our weekly meals at home. The leafy greens are full of vitamins, minerals, antioxidants, fiber, and calcium. For variation, you can swap the spinach for broccoli or another leafy green vegetable.

85g (12oz) whole-wheat pasta (spaghetti or your favorite kind)

1 head spinach

2 large, vine-ripened, organic tomatoes

1 head garlic

Olive oil

1 teaspoon red pepper flakes

Freshly ground sea salt and pepper

1 lemon

Parmesan cheese, for garnish

Organic mixed salad leaves

½ red onion, chopped

1. Boil the spaghetti for five minutes or until almost cooked—al dente. Drain, reserving 60ml (2fl oz) of the water.

2. Rinse and chop the spinach and tomatoes. Chop the garlic and sauté over medium-high heat in a little olive oil until golden brown.

3. Slowly add the spinach to the olive oil and garlic, stirring as you go. Turn the heat down to medium and add the 60ml (2fl oz) of pasta water and the pepper flakes. Stir, then cover for three minutes.

4. Add the chopped tomatoes, the pepper, and a dash of sea salt. Stir and add the juice of half a lemon. Cover, turn the heat down to low, and simmer for 15 minutes.

5. Turn off the heat and mix in the pasta. Serve topped with freshly grated parmesan and pepper.

6. Assemble the salad leaves with one-quarter of a thinly sliced red onion. Top with freshly ground pepper and a dash of sea salt. Add 1 tablespoon of olive oil and the juice from the other half of the lemon. Toss and serve.

Pan-Seared Flounder with Roasted Brussels Sprouts and Sautéed Kale

SERVES FOUR

It's hard to beat fresh flounder! It's a light, flaky fish without a lot of fishy flavor. Paired with Brussels sprouts and kale, it really tastes terrific!

Olive oil
900g (2lb) fresh wild flounder, washed
    and dried, cut into 4 pieces
Freshly ground pepper
1 lemon
3 medium-sized organic carrots
200g (8oz) organic Brussels sprouts
25g (1oz) walnuts
Organic kale, one bunch
6 cloves garlic
Sea salt

1. Heat a little olive oil in a stovetop pan. Place the flounder in the oil and sprinkle with freshly ground pepper. Add freshly squeezed lemon to taste. Cook each side for three to four minutes, or until golden brown, over medium-high heat.

2. Preheat oven to 220°C (425°F/Gas Mark 7). Wash and slice the carrots and cut the Brussels sprouts in half. Chop the walnuts. Combine everything in a large pan with the olive oil and bake for 35 minutes. Stir as needed.

3. Rinse and chop the kale and chop the garlic. Sauté the garlic in olive oil over medium-high heat, add the kale, and cook until golden brown. Stir and add freshly ground pepper and sea salt.

➡ Baby Butter Beans

SERVES FOUR

160g (5 ½oz) sweet onion, finely chopped
1 stalk celery, finely chopped
450g (1lb) butter beans
1 tablespoon olive oil
Sea salt
Freshly ground pepper

1. In a saucepan, cover the sweet onion and celery with filtered water. Bring to a slow boil. Cook about 5 minutes.

2. Pour the butter beans in with onions and celery. Cover with water. Cook 45 minutes on low heat until beans are tender.

3. Season with 1 tablespoon of olive oil and a sprinkle of sea salt and freshly ground pepper.

→ Spring Greens

SERVES THREE TO FOUR

1 head spring greens
Olive oil
2 teaspoons white wine vinegar
   or sweet pickles

1. Choose a fresh green head of spring greens. Using kitchen shears, cut off leaves and rinse well. The heavy leaf stems may be cut out and leaves chopped in small pieces. Saute these in a light coating of olive oil.

2. After leaves are limp, add a small amount of filtered water and steam about 20 minutes until leaves are tender.

3. Season with 2 teaspoons white wine vinegar or sweet pickles.

And When I Feel Like Baking!...

↠ Apple Crumble

SERVES THREE TO FOUR

This isn't just a tasty, healthy dessert—it's also a great breakfast treat! Use leftover crumble as a topping for porridge on Sunday morning—it's incredible!

4 medium-sized Bramley apples
1 lemon
2 tablespoons butter
1 tablespoon olive oil
2 tablespoons dark brown sugar
25g (1oz) rolled oats or unsweetened muesli
25g (1oz) chopped pecans

1. Wash and slice the apples. Cover with the juice of the lemon.

2. Melt the butter in a saucepan and add in the olive oil, brown sugar, and oats. Remove from the heat and mix with a fork. Add pecans.

3. Coat the apples with the crumble mixture and transfer to a baking pan. Bake for 35 minutes at 190°C (375°F/ Gas Mark 5).

The Ballet Beautiful Friends and Family Recipes

I love sharing healthy recipes and tips with my Ballet Beauties! Below are some of my favorites that they have shared with me.

⟶ John's Vegetarian Chili Recipe

SERVES FOUR TO SIX

My older brother John is a terrific chef. Everything that he cooks is great but I especially love his veggie chili on days when it is cold outside! He serves it with cornbread, but when I make it at home I generally serve it with a salad and whole-grain bread. One pot will last several days.

Olive oil
1 large onion, diced
1 red or orange pepper, diced
4 or 5 cloves garlic, chopped
1 can black beans, drained
1 can kidney beans, drained
1 can diced tomatoes
1 can stewed Mexican tomatoes
    (jalapeños, garlic, cumin), mashed
1 can vegetable broth
1 packet chili mix
Cumin (optional)
Chili powder (optional)
Black pepper (*Note:* John and I don't
    measure—we estimate!)

1. Heat the olive oil on medium-high heat, add the onion, and sauté for two minutes. Add the diced pepper and cook for another three or four minutes, until the pepper is soft. Add the garlic and cook for another 30 to 60 seconds, until the garlic is fragrant. Add the beans, tomatoes, broth, and chili mix. Cook on medium high until the chili starts to boil. Reduce heat to medium.

2. If the chili is too runny, cook uncovered. If it seems perfect, turn the heat down low and cook covered. (Chili can scorch, so don't cook it on too high a heat). I find that there isn't enough flavor from one package of chili mix, so add cumin, chili powder, and black pepper to taste. Cook for 20 to 30 minutes. Chili does seem to get better the longer it simmers.

3. This recipe is really flexible. For example, you don't have to use two kinds of tomatoes—they can both be diced plain tomatoes or they can both be stewed tomatoes. Think your chili needs more tomatoes? Add another can. If you like a little heat, add some chopped jalapeños. Don't want to use a packet of chili mix? Make up your own spice mix—chili, cumin, oregano, garlic powder, onion powder, etc. Cooking like this is an art, not a science. Do whatever you like best! Maybe add some chipotle peppers to give your chili that smokiness. Beer adds great flavor too—just pour some in!

➻ Romy's Lentil Soup

SERVES FOUR TO SIX

Romy swears that Ballet Beautiful and her lentil soup were the keys to her incredible post-baby Ballet Beautiful body! I'm making her soup now, and I love it too!

Olive oil
1 yellow onion, chopped
1 teaspoon sea salt
3 or 4 carrots, chopped
2/3 bunch celery, chopped
2 organic vegan stock cubes
Sea salt
Cayenne
Turmeric
Coriander
450g (1lb) French lentils, rinsed
Bay leaves
Kale (lacinato or your favorite)

1. Add some olive oil and the chopped yellow onion to a large soup pot at medium heat. Sprinkle with the sea salt and let the onion sweat down.

2. Add the carrots and celery. Let everything cook down on medium heat. Add the vegan stock cube, sea salt, some cayenne, a couple of dashes of turmeric, and some coriander.

3. Add the French lentils and a few bay leaves to the pot and cover with water. Let everything cook down. Keep watching and stir occasionally.

4. After the lentils have cooked until soft (about a half-hour), add the kale.

5. When the soup is almost finished, add a heavy drizzle of good extra-virgin olive oil to the pot for richness and flavor. You can even add a tiny drizzle when serving and a tiny pinch of sea salt to taste. Enjoy!

↠ Ashley's Baked Kale Snack

SERVES TWO

This is one of my favorite snacks. It's super-easy to make and really nutritious too!

1 head kale (any type you prefer), washed and completely dried
1–2 tablespoons olive oil
Sea salt

1. Cut the kale up into big pieces and toss it with the olive oil until the leaves are coated. Spread the kale on a baking sheet.

2. Bake at 180°C (350°F/Gas Mark 4) for 15 to 20 minutes, or until crispy. Remove from the oven and lightly sprinkle with sea salt.

⇝ Eliza's Toasted Snack

SERVES TWO

My friend Eliza's toast recipe, a favorite with her daughter, is great for a quick and satisfying snack or as a side along with vegetable soup for lunch. For a touch of something sweet, add a little honey on top.

Multigrain bread
Extra-virgin olive oil
Sea salt

1. Take several slices of a multigrain bread and lay them out on a baking sheet. Sprinkle some good-quality extra-virgin olive oil over the bread slices, then sprinkle on some sea salt.

2. Heat the bread at 100–130°C (200–250°F) until it's soft and warm, usually 10 minutes.

3. Cut up the slices and enjoy a great snack!

→ My Dad's Deviled Eggs

SERVES FOUR

I borrowed this one from my father—it's a classic southern snack! Perfect for a cocktail or tailgate party, deviled eggs provide lots of protein without a lot of extra calories and fat. I love them so much that I served them with pink champagne at the cocktail hour at our wedding!

6 hard-boiled eggs, peeled
1 tablespoon spicy brown mustard
60g (2oz) reduced-fat mayonnaise with
    olive oil
1 teaspoon white vinegar
2 tablespoons sweet pickle relish
Paprika

1. Cut the peeled eggs lengthwise in half. Remove the yolks into a bowl. Set the egg white sections aside.

2. Mash the yolks with a fork. Add the mustard, mayonnaise, vinegar, and pickle relish and stir until well mixed.

3. Using either a fork or spoon, stuff the egg white halves with the yolk mixture. Sprinkle each egg half lightly with paprika.

David's Quick Prawn Saganaki with Sun-Dried Tomatoes

My brother David doesn't eat meat. He loves seafood, and this is one of his favorites. I love this simplified version of a super-tasty Greek dish.

- 225–340g (8–12oz) jar of sun-dried tomatoes in oil
- 170g (6oz) feta cheese in brine
- 2–3 pinches (to taste) fresh herbs such as parsley, basil, oregano, thyme, and dill
- 450g (1lb) shelled, deveined prawns
- ½ lemon (optional)

1. Chop the sun-dried tomatoes and feta cheese into small pieces.

2. Chop the fresh herbs very fine. Mix the tomato mixture, herbs and prawns and place in a baking dish. Note that some oil from the sun-dried tomatoes will mix with the dish. (This is a good thing!)

3. Bake at 190°C (375°F/Gas Mark 5) for 20 minutes, or until prawns are cooked and pink. Squeeze lemon juice over the top. Serve over pasta, over rice, or with bread.

→ Suzanne's Baked Fish with Garlic and Ginger

Suzanne is a busy mother of five. She shared this recipe with me as the feature of one of her go-to healthy meals. Combine it with a green salad or sautéed or steamed greens and a baked sweet potato and you have a powerhouse healthy meal! And it's delicious—like eating out but healthier and cheaper.

Put into a food processor:

½ teaspoon fresh ginger root

2 cloves garlic

2 green onions

50g (2oz) coriander

2 tablespoons olive oil

4 teaspoons maple syrup

1. Spread this mixture on top of the fish in a slightly oiled pan.

2. Sprinkle with salt. Put aluminum foil over the pan.

3. Bake at 200°C (400°F/Gas Mark 6) for about 30 minutes.

Carrie's Healthy Fruit and Spinach Salad

SERVES FOUR

I never get tired of my mom Carrie's fruit and spinach salad because it changes with the season or the fruit on hand. And it's beautiful, delicious, and healthy!

120ml (4fl oz) white wine vinegar

5 tablespoons spicy mustard

2 tablespoons maple syrup

2 bunches fresh spinach

2 or more fruits of the season, such as apples and bananas, peaches and blueberries, or oranges and pears

225g (8oz) small fresh mozzarella balls, halved

Chopped walnuts

1. For the dressing, mix the white wine vinegar, spicy mustard, and maple syrup. (You can substitute honey if you prefer, though the taste of maple syrup blends in better.) Shake well, and add more of any of the three ingredients to taste. Refrigerate for use anytime!

2. Dress the spinach with the dressing and add fruits.

3. Top with the mozzarella and walnuts.

Elizabeth's Prawn Creole

SERVES SIX

Elizabeth grew up on the coast of North Carolina. I love the mix of flavors in her healthy prawn creole and how great it makes me feel! She passed along this recipe from a 1975 cookbook entitled *Seafood Cookery from Carteret County Kitchens*.

450g (1lb) fresh prawns

35g (1 ¼oz) onion, chopped

45g (1 ½oz) green pepper, chopped

25g (1oz) celery, chopped

1 clove garlic, chopped fine

250ml (2fl oz) olive oil or 55g (2oz) butter

1 teaspoon chili powder

Dash of black pepper

1 bay leaf

1 teaspoon salt

725g (1lb 9 ½oz) fresh tomatoes, diced

1. Peel the prawns and wash them. Cut the large prawns in half.

2. Cook the onion, green pepper, celery, and garlic in oil until tender.

3. Blend in the seasonings. Add the tomatoes and cook until thick, stirring constantly.

4. Add the prawns and simmer uncovered for about 20 minutes. Serve over cooked brown rice.

→ Baked Sweet Potatoes

This is a classic family recipe that pairs really well with my butterbean recipe (on page 227) and fish.

1. Place a glass pie plate filled with water on the bottom rack of the oven. Preheat oven to 200°C (400°F/Gas Mark 6).

2. Wash six to eight red sweet potatoes and place them on a baking sheet, making sure they do not touch.

3. Cook 45 minutes in the oven.

4. Without opening the oven, turn the heat down to 190°C (375°F/Gas Mark 5) and continue baking for another 30 minutes.

5. Still not opening the oven, turn the heat to 160°C (325°F/Gas Mark 3) for 15 minutes. Turn off the oven and leave the potatoes in the oven for 10 more minutes.

6. Store cooked, unpeeled potatoes by placing them in a large ziplock plastic bag. Take out, peel, and heat as needed. The potatoes can also be peeled, mashed, and used in casseroles and pies. They keep well for a week in the refrigerator.

All of these recipes are great options for healthy, delicious meals that you can enjoy as you sculpt your Ballet Beautiful body! If you don't always have access to a kitchen to make them at home, study the ingredients and look for similar options when eating out. I can't wait to hear how you like them!

A Final Note

Ballet Beautiful is more than a fitness method or a workout program—it is an inspired lifestyle that supports a life of health, balance, and beauty. It's one that is constantly evolving too. Your body and your mind will go through many exciting transformations and changes on the program as you dig in deep and really connect with it. I know Ballet Beautiful has changed my own life—in fact, it is the greatest thing that has ever happened to me! Ballet Beautiful has given me confidence, health, and a level of strength I never would have dreamed possible. All of this while allowing me to be both feminine and strong. I'm empowered by the Ballet Beautiful mindset, and I know that you will be too.

I am delighted to welcome you to our growing global community as I share with you in this book all that I have discovered. I cannot wait to hear about your own experiences and incredible results. Please become part of the growing worldwide Ballet Beautiful community at *www.balletbeautiful.com*, where you can become a member, take live online classes, sign up for my blog, and stay updated on new exercises. (I create them all the time!) You can also follow me on Twitter @balletbeautiful and on Facebook at Ballet Beautiful. Not only will staying connected with Ballet Beautiful reinforce your success, but you will feel part of something much bigger than yourself!

Thank you for joining me on what I hope will be an incredible and long-lasting trip toward greater health, happiness, and success!

Welcome to Ballet Beautiful and enjoy!

Love! xoxo Mary Helen

ACKNOWLEDGMENTS

Ballet Beautiful is built on a foundation of incredible support and love. My thanks go to the many wonderful people in my life who helped me create this program and to everyone who helped me write and publish my first book!

First, my family: Thank you to my parents for their love—for letting me move to New York at 15 to pursue my crazy dream of being a ballerina and for cheering me on every step of the way! My love goes to Paul, my husband, for supporting me and Ballet Beautiful every day and for teaching me how to swim the crawl and buying me dark chocolate!

And my colleagues: To Billie Fitzpatrick, my wonderful collaborator, thanks for your guidance at every turn and for your terrific patience in my pursuit of perfection! I am grateful to Matthew Elblonk, my meticulous agent at De Fiore, and to Renee, the world's kindest and most engaging editor, and her fabulous team at Da Capo Press for bringing this book to life! And to the incredible Yelena Yemchuck: my deepest appreciation for conveying Ballet Beautiful through your beautiful images! Costanza Theodoli-Braschi, thank you for the beautiful illustrations of the basic ballet positions. And of course, I treasure my amazing team at Ballet Beautiful! Julie helps me make it happen every day, and Ashley brings my vision to life on the screen.

And friends: A huge thank-you to Natalie for the beautiful foreword to this book and a thousand hours of her hard work, incredible kindness, and all-around awesomeness. Thanks to my first Ballet Beauties: Sarah, Romy, Rain, Karen, Zooey, Chelsea, Kate, Liv,

Leith, Kirsten, Eliza, Evgenia, Kristina, Rachel, Cora, Tracee, and Lynn, and to Gina, Rose, Katie, Val, Filipa, Helena, and all of the BB girls . . . I am so inspired by you all!!

I would like to give a special hug to everyone who was there at the beginning of this exciting ride! Carlos and Andrea, Linda, Dave, Tom, John and Alicia, Heather, Jeff, Laura and Patrick—thank you all.

And a final expression of thanks to you and the thousands of others who have taken a small leap to try Ballet Beautiful. I am humbled that you invite me into your daily lives to share my exercise and wellness program and hope you find in it reward and happiness for many years to come.

INDEX

The Recipe index starts on page 249.

Mary Helen Bowers is a professional ballerina and the founder and CEO of Ballet Beautiful. Originally from Charlotte, North Carolina, Mary Helen moved to New York City at age 15 to attend the School of American Ballet and pursue her dream of dancing as a professional ballerina. She was invited to join New York City Ballet the following year and went on to dance 10 years with the company at Lincoln Center and on stages across the world.

After retiring from New York City Ballet, Mary Helen went on to earn her Bachelor of Arts degree in English Literature from Columbia University. Upon graduating in 2008 she launched Ballet Beautiful, a ballet-inspired fitness and wellness company that shares the artistry, athleticism and inherent grace of ballet with other women around the world.

As a tech-savvy entrepreneur, Mary Helen has grown Ballet Beautiful to reach a now-international membership, and has been acclaimed by many, including: *Elle, Vogue, Women's Health, Harper's Bazaar, CNN, ABC,* the *New York Times*, and the *Wall Street Journal.*

Mary Helen lives with her husband in New York City.

For more information, and to check out online classes and Ballet Beautiful videos and DVDs, please visit www.balletbeautiful.com